Frommer's®

P9-CCA-355

Maui
day BY day™

2nd Edition

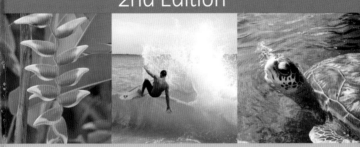

by Jeanette Foster

WILEY

Wiley Publishing, Inc.

Contents

Published by:
Wiley Publishing, Inc.

111 River St.
Hoboken, NJ 07030-5774

ISBN 978-0-470-49763-0

Editor: Jamie Ehrlich
Production Editors: Heather Wilcox, Lindsay Conner & Michael Brumitt
Photo Editor: Richard Fox
Cartographer: Andrew Dolan
Production by Wiley Indianapolis Composition Services

For information on our other products and services or to obtain technical support, please contact our Customer Care Department within the U.S. at 877/762-2974, outside the U.S. at 317/572-3993 or fax 317/572-4002.

Wiley also publishes its books in a variety of electronic formats. Some content that appears in print may not be available in electronic formats.

Manufactured in China

5   4   3   2   1

A Note from the Editorial Director

Organizing your time. That's what this guide is all about.

Other guides give you long lists of things to see and do and then expect you to fit the pieces together. The Day by Day guides are different. These guides tell you the best of everything, and then they show you how to see it *in the smartest, most time-efficient way*. Our authors have designed detailed itineraries organized by time, neighborhood, or special interest. And each tour comes with a bulleted map that takes you from stop to stop.

Hoping to sunbathe on a secluded beach, or to explore Haleakala National Park? Planning on snorkeling Molokini, driving the winding road to Hana, or relaxing at one of Maui's beachside spas? Whatever your interest or schedule, the Day by Days give you the smartest routes to follow. Not only do we take you to the top attractions, hotels, and restaurants, but we also help you access those special moments that locals get to experience—those "finds" that turn tourists into travelers.

The Day by Days are also your top choice if you're looking for one complete guide for all your travel needs. The best hotels and restaurants for every budget, the greatest shopping values, the wildest nightlife—it's all here.

Why should you trust our judgment? Because our authors personally visit each place they write about. They're an independent lot who say what they think and would never include places they wouldn't recommend to their best friends. They're also open to suggestions from readers. If you'd like to contact them, please send your comments our way at feedback@frommers.com, and we'll pass them on.

Enjoy your Day by Day guide—the most helpful travel companion you can buy. And have the trip of a lifetime.

Warm regards,

Kelly Regan, Editorial Director
Frommer's Travel Guides

About the Author

A resident of the Big Island, **Jeanette Foster** has skied the slopes of Mauna Kea—during a Fourth of July ski meet, no less—and gone scuba diving with manta rays off the Kona Coast. A prolific writer widely published in travel, sports, and adventure magazines, she's also the editor of *Zagat's Survey to Hawaii's Top Restaurants*. In addition to writing this guide, Jeanette is the author of *Frommer's Hawaii Day by Day, Frommer's Hawaii, Frommer's Maui, Frommer's Hawaii from $80 a Day, Frommer's Honolulu, Waikiki & Oahu, Frommer's Kauai, Frommer's Hawaii with Kids, Frommer's Portable Big Island,* and *Frommer's Honolulu, Waikiki & Oahu.*

An Additional Note

Please be advised that travel information is subject to change at any time—and this is especially true of prices. We therefore suggest that you write or call ahead for confirmation when making your travel plans. The authors, editors, and publisher cannot be held responsible for the experiences of readers while traveling. Your safety is important to us, however, so we encourage you to stay alert and be aware of your surroundings.

Star Ratings, Icons & Abbreviations

Every hotel, restaurant, and attraction listing in this guide has been ranked for quality, value, service, amenities, and special features using a **star-rating system.** Hotels, restaurants, attractions, shopping, and nightlife are rated on a scale of zero stars (recommended) to three stars (exceptional). In addition to the star-rating system, we also use a **kids icon** to point out the best bets for families. Within each tour, we recommend cafes, bars, or restaurants where you can take a break. Each of these stops appears in a shaded box marked with a coffee-cup-shaped bullet ☕ .

The following **abbreviations** are used for credit cards:

AE	American Express	DISC	Discover	V	Visa
DC	Diners Club	MC	MasterCard		

Frommers.com

Now that you have this guidebook to help you plan a great trip, visit our website at **www.frommers.com** for additional travel information on more than 4,000 destinations. We update features regularly to give you instant access to the most current trip-planning information available. At Frommers.com, you'll find scoops on the best airfares, lodging rates, and car rental bargains. You can even book your travel online through our reliable travel booking partners. Other popular features include:

- Online updates of our most popular guidebooks
- Vacation sweepstakes and contest giveaways
- Newsletters highlighting the hottest travel trends
- Podcasts, interactive maps, and up-to-the-minute events listings
- Opinionated blog entries by Arthur Frommer himself
- Online travel message boards with featured travel discussions

A Note on Prices

In the "Take a Break" and "Best Bets" sections of this book, we have used a system of dollar signs to show a range of costs for 1 night in a hotel (the price of a double-occupancy room) or the cost of an entree at a restaurant. Use the following table to decipher the dollar signs:

Cost	Hotels	Restaurants
$	under $130	under $10
$$	$130–$200	$10–$20
$$$	$200–$300	$20–$30
$$$$	$300–$395	$30–$40
$$$$$	over $395	over $40

An Invitation to the Reader

In researching this book, we discovered many wonderful places—hotels, restaurants, shops, and more. We're sure you'll find others. Please tell us about them, so we can share the information with your fellow travelers in upcoming editions. If you were disappointed with a recommendation, we'd love to know that, too. Please write to:

Frommer's Maui Day by Day, 2nd Edition
Wiley Publishing, Inc. • 111 River St. • Hoboken, NJ 07030-5774

16 Favorite **Moments**

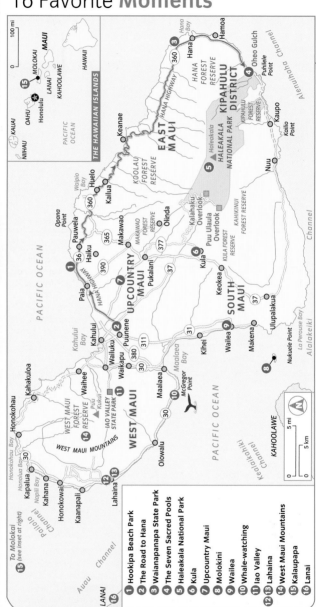

Previous page: Napili Beach, looking toward Molokai Island.

To experience the true magic of Maui, just step outside to watch the glow of a sunrise, see the reflection of the moon on the inky ocean, sniff the perfume of flowers dancing in the air, or listen to the murmur of a tropical breeze through a bamboo forest. A few more of my favorite Maui experiences are described below.

Top surfer Laird Hamilton (left) at Hookipa Beach.

① **Watching windsurfers ride the waves at Hookipa.** This beach draws windsurfers and surfers from around the globe to ride, sail, and pirouette over the waves. Watching them flip into the air while rotating 360 degrees is the best free show in town. *See p 76.*

② **Smelling the sweet scent of ginger on the road to Hana.** At every twist on this windy road you are greeted by exotic tropical blossoms, thundering waterfalls, breathtaking vistas, and a glimpse at what Maui looked like before it was "discovered." *See p 64.*

③ **Walking the shoreline trail at Waianapanapa.** This trail will take you back in time, past lava cliffs, a tropical forest, an ancient *heiau* (temple), mysterious caves, an exploding blowhole, native Hawaiian plants, and the ever-changing sea. *See p 69.*

④ **Taking a dip in the Seven Sacred Pools.** These fern-shrouded waterfall pools spill seaward at Oheo Gulch, on the rain-shrouded eastern flanks of Haleakala. *See p 71.*

⑤ **Greeting the rising sun from atop Haleakala.** Dress warmly and drive the 37 miles (60km) from sea level up to 10,000 feet (3,048m), where you can watch the sunrise. Breathing in the rarefied air and watching the first rays of light streak across the sky is a mystical experience. *See p 84.*

⑥ **Heading to Kula to bid the sun aloha.** This town perched on the side of Haleakala is the perfect place to watch the sun set over the entire island, with vistas across the isthmus, the West Maui Mountains, and Molokai and Lanai in the distance. *See p 63.*

⑦ **Exploring upcountry Maui.** On the slopes of Haleakala, cowboys, farmers, ranchers, and other country people make their serene, neighborly homes, worlds away from the bustling beach resorts. *See p 62.*

⑧ **Snorkeling off Molokini.** Calm, protected waters in the islet's crater, plus an abundance of marine life, make Molokini one of Hawaii's best places to snorkel. Paddle with turtles, watch clouds of butterflyfish

A beachside massage is the perfect way to relax.

flitter past, and search for tiny damselfish in the coral. *See p 101.*

9 Pampering in paradise. Maui's spas have raised the art of relaxation and healing to a new level. A massage on the beach will sooth out the kinks, while you bask in the sounds of the ocean, smell the salt air, and feel the caress of a warm breeze. *See p 36.*

10 Watching for whales. From mid-December through the end of March, humpback whales can be seen from shore jumping, breaching, and slapping their pectoral fins. *See p 105.*

11 Exploring Iao Valley. When the sun strikes Iao Valley in the West Maui Mountains, an almost ethereal light sends rays out in all directions. This really may be Eden. *See p 60.*

12 Visiting a historic port town. In the 1800s, whalers swarmed into Lahaina and missionaries fought to stem the spread of their sinful influence. Rediscover those wild whaling days for yourself. *See p 50.*

Lahaina Harbor.

13 Experiencing Art Night in Lahaina. Every Friday, under a canopy of stars, the town's galleries open their doors and serve refreshments. Wander in to see what's going on in Maui's creative community. *See p 136.*

14 Flying over the remote West Maui Mountains. The only way to see the inaccessible, prehistoric West Maui Mountains is by helicopter. You'll fly low over razor-thin cliffs and flutter past sparkling waterfalls while descending into canyons and valleys. *See p 20.*

15 Riding a mule to Kalaupapa. Even if you have only 1 day to spend on Molokai, spend it on a mule. Trek from "topside" Molokai down a narrow, dizzying switchback trail to Kalaupapa National Historic Park below. *See p 20.*

16 Taking a day trip to Lanai. Sailing from Lahaina Harbor, you can admire Maui from offshore, go snorkeling in the clear waters of Lanai, tour this tiny former plantation island, and still catch the last ferry back. *See p 149.* ●

1 Strategies for Seeing **Maui**

Strategies for Seeing **Maui**

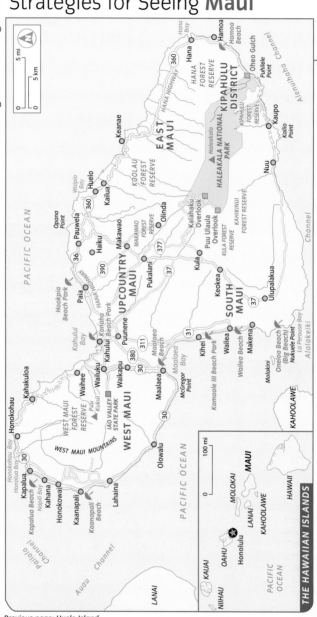

5 mi

5 km

Hana Bay

360

Hana

Hamoa

Hamoa Beach

Oheo Gulch

HANA FOREST RESERVE

KIPAHULU DISTRICT

Puhilele Point

Alenuihaha Channel

HANA HIGHWAY

Keanae

EAST MAUI

HALEAKALA NATIONAL PARK

KIPAHULU FOREST RESERVE

Kaupo

Kalio Point

KOOLAU FOREST RESERVE

Haleakala

KAHIKINUI FOREST RESERVE

Waipio Bay

Huelo

360

Kailua

Opana Point

Pauwela

36

Haiku

Olinda

Kalahaku Overlook

Puu Ulaula Overlook

Nuu

PACIFIC OCEAN

HANA HIGHWAY

390

Makawao

MAKAWAO FOREST RESERVE

377

KULA FOREST RESERVE

Hookipa Beach Park

Paia

Kahulu Beach Park

UPCOUNTRY MAUI

Pukalani

37

Kula

Keokea

Kahului Bay

Waikapu

Puunene

311

Keokea

Ulupalakua

37

SOUTH MAUI

Kahakuloa

Waihee

Wailuku

30

380

Maalaea

31

31

Kihei

Wailea

Makena

WEST MAUI FOREST RESERVE

Puu Kukui

IAO VALLEY STATE PARK

Maalaea Bay

McGregor Point

Kamaole III Beach Park

Wailea Beach

Oneloa Beach (Big Beach)

Nukele Point

La Perouse Bay

Alalakeiki

WEST MAUI MOUNTAINS

WEST MAUI

30

Molokini

Honokohau

Honokohau Bay

Honolua Bay

30

Kapalua

Kapalua Beach

Napili Bay

Kahana

Honokowai

Kaanapali

Kaanapali Beach

Lahaina

Olowalu

30

KAHOOLAWE

Pailolo Channel

PACIFIC OCEAN

Auau Channel

100 mi

MAUI

MOLOKAI

LANAI

KAHOOLAWE

HAWAII

KAUAI

OAHU

Honolulu

NIIHAU

LANAI

PACIFIC OCEAN

THE HAWAIIAN ISLANDS

Previous page: Huelo Island.

You've probably traveled a long way to get to Maui, and your vacation time is precious. There really is just one cardinal rule: relax. Maui is not a place to "see" but a place to experience. If you are too busy rushing to see everything, you won't experience the magic of the island. Here are my suggestions for making the most out of your time.

Rule #1: Remember you are on vacation

Don't jam your days with activities; allow time to relax, to stop and smell the plumerias. Since you'll probably arrive jet-lagged, make sure to spend some time on your first day lounging at the beach or the hotel swimming pool. Don't forget that exposure to sunlight can help reset your internal clock—another good reason to visit the beach when you arrive.

Take some time to stop and smell the plumerias.

Rule #2: Driving takes a lot longer on Maui

You will need a car to get around; Maui does not have adequate public transportation. But plan to get out of your car as much as possible. Don't just look at Maui from the car window; get out and breathe in the tropical aroma, soak in those views, and listen to the sounds of the island. Sure, you could drive the 50-mile-long (80km) Hana Highway in as few as 2 to 3 hours, but that would miss the point of the journey entirely. One last thing: Maui does have traffic jams. From 7 to 9am and 4 to 6pm the main roads are bumper-to-bumper with commuters. Plan accordingly. Sleep in late and get on the road after the traffic has cleared out, or watch the sunset and then go to dinner.

Rule #3: If your visit is short, stay in one place

Unless you're visiting for a week or longer, try not to hotel hop. With the exception of Hana, all the towns on Maui are within easy driving distance. Second, it is not easy (or cheap) checking in and out of hotels. There's the schlepping of the luggage (and the corresponding tips to the parking valet, the bellman, and so on), the waiting in line to check in, and unpacking, only to

Maluaka Beach.

Strategies for Seeing Maui

Fly Direct

If possible, fly nonstop and directly to the island of Maui (the airport is in Kahului and the airport code is OGG). Not only is it easier, but it will also save you time. Yes, there are flights from the U.S. mainland through Honolulu and then on to Maui, but the "on to Maui" bit generally means getting off a plane in the big, big Honolulu International Airport and transferring to another terminal. Going through the fun-filled security procedures (taking off your shoes again!) and then checking in and waiting (sometimes up to 2 hr.) for your flight to Maui is no way to begin a vacation.

repeat the entire process a few days later. Your vacation time is too precious.

Rule #4: Pick the key activity of the day and plan accordingly

To maximize your time, decide what you really want to do that day, then plan all other activities in the same geographical area. For example, if you really want to go golfing at Kapalua, pick a beach in the same area for the afternoon or a shopping spree in the area and plan dinner nearby, that way you won't have to trek back and forth across the island. Take some time to stop and smell the plumerias.

Rule #5: Remember you are on the island of aloha

Maui is different. Slow down (no need to rush, you're on vacation). Smile and say "aloha." It's what the local residents do. Ask them: "How-zit?" (the local expression for "how are you?"). When they ask you, tell 'em, "Couldn't be better—I'm on Maui!" Wave at everyone—you'll feel better, they'll feel better. Laugh a lot, even if things aren't going as planned—laugh. Even if you're stuck in a traffic jam—laugh. (Hey, you're on Maui, how bad can it be?)

Rule #6: Use this book as a reference, not a concrete plan

You will not hurt my feelings if you don't follow every single tour and do absolutely everything I've suggested. In fact, you'll have a better time if you pick and choose the tours you want to take and the things you want to do. This book is filled with recommendations. ●

Keep your eyes peeled, and you might see a Hawaiian honeycreeper like this one.

The Best in Three Days

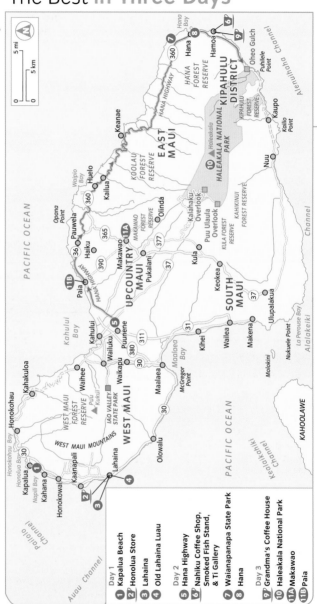

Day 1
1 Kapalua Beach
2 Honolua Store
3 Lahaina
4 Old Lahaina Luau

Day 2
5 Hana Highway
6 Nahiku Coffee Shop, Smoked Fish Stand, & Ti Gallery
7 Waianapanapa State Park
8 Hana

Day 3
9 Grandma's Coffee House
10 Haleakala National Park
11A Makawao
11B Paia

Previous page: Haleakala National Park.

aui may be an island, but it's a big one (48 miles×26 miles/77km×42km), the second largest of the Hawaiian Islands. If you only have 3 days, concentrate on the very best Maui has to offer: a beach, the scenic Hana Highway, and the view from the top of Haleakala, a 10,000-foot-high (3,048km) dormant volcano. Try to spend your first night in conveniently located Lahaina/Kaanapali. Day 1 from the airport to your accommodations in Lahaina/Kaanapali and to the beach is 40 miles (64km); Day 2 to Hana is 75 miles (121km); and Day 3, from Hana to Haleakala and back to the airport, is 87 miles (140km). START: **Kapalua Beach. Trip length: 177-mile (285km) loop.**

Travel Tip

For detailed descriptions of the beaches in this chapter, see chapter 5. For hotel reviews, see chapter 7. For more on the recommended restaurants, see chapter 8.

To get to Kapalua Beach from Lahaina/Kaanapali, take Hwy. 30 north to Kapalua. Go left at the Kapalua Resort sign onto Office Road and follow it to the end. Take a left on Honoapiilai Road and a right at the beach access sign next-door to the Napili Kai condominium.

1 ★★★ **Kapalua Beach.** Check in to your hotel, then head for Kapalua Beach. Don't overdo the sun on your first day. Bring plenty of water, sunscreen, and a hat. The adventurous might want to rent snorkel equipment, but those seeking a relaxing afternoon should simply lounge on the sand and enjoy the warm water. *See p 77.*

Retrace your route back to Hwy. 30 and turn right; continue into Lahaina town.

2 **Honolua Store.** For a quick sandwich or a cold drink, I love this old-fashioned country general store, with surprisingly low prices. *502 Office Rd., just after the entrance to*

Luxuriating in the warm sea and sun of Kapalua Beach.

the Ritz-Carlton Kapalua ☎ *808/669-6128. $.*

3 ★★ **Lahaina.** After an hour or two at the beach, spend a couple of hours walking this historic old town, which at one time was the capital of Hawaii, a favorite spot for both whalers and missionaries. Today, not only can you enjoy the oceanfront village's historical past, but also its unique boutique shops, dozens of restaurants, and nightlife spots. *See the walking tour on p 50 for more information.*

Boats moored in Lahaina Harbor.

4 ★★★ **Old Lahaina Luau.** To really feel as though you are in Hawaii, attend this sunset luau and immerse yourself in the local culture. The luau begins at sunset and features Tahitian and Hawaiian entertainment. The food is as much Pacific Rim as authentically Hawaiian, from imu-roasted kalua pig to baked mahimahi to teriyaki sirloin steak. *1251 Front St.* ☎ *800/248-5828 or 808/667-1998. www.old lahainaluau.com. $89 adults, $59 children 12 and under. See p 124.*

From Lahaina/Kaanapali take Hwy. 30 south to Hwy. 380 and turn right (east). In Kahului Hwy. 380 becomes Dairy Road. Turn right (east) on Hwy. 36.

5 ★★★ **Hana Highway.** You'll probably wake up early on your first full day in Hawaii, so take advantage of it and get out as quickly as you can and onto the scenic Hana Highway. Allow at least 3½ to 5 hours for the journey. Pull over often, get out to take photos, smell the flowers, and jump in the mountain-stream pools. Wave to everyone, move off the road for those speeding by, and breathe in Hawaii. *For a detailed description of this route, see p 64.*

After MM 16, Hwy. 36 becomes Hwy. 360 and starts with MM 0. After about 1 to 1½ hours down the road, a ½ mile (.8km) past MM 28, you'll see:

6 **Nahiku Coffee Shop.** This small coffee shop sells delicious locally made baked goods, Maui-grown coffee, banana bread, organic tropical-fruit smoothies, and the Original and Best Coconut Candy made by Hana character Jungle Johnny.

Another 20 minutes down the road, just past MM 32 is:

7 **Waianapanapa State Park.** Just outside of Hana, stop at this state park and take a hike along the black-sand beach. *See p 89.*

About ½ mile (.8km) after MM 33 you come to the outskirts of Hana; veer left at the police and fire station onto Ua Kea Road.

8 **Hana.** While you're here, make sure to hit three of my favorite spots, the **Hana Cultural Center and Museum,** the **Hasagawa General Store,** and **Hana Coast Gallery.** Spend the night in Hana. *For more detailed information on Hana's sights, see p 68.*

Allow at least 2 hours to get from Hana to the top of Haleakala.

The dramatic black sands of Waianapanapa State Park.

Maui Driving Tips

Hawaii residents know the highways by their Hawaiian names; very few know the highway numbers. I've included both the Hawaiian highway name and number on the maps, but the directions in this book mainly refer to the highway number. You'll also see the abbreviation MM, which stands for "mile marker." Below is a quick reference to the names and numbers of Maui's highways.

Hwy. 30: Honoapiilani Highway
Hwy. 31: Piilani Highway
Hwy. 36 and Hwy. 360: Hana Highway
Hwy. 37: Haleakala Highway and the Kula Highway
Hwy. 311: Mokulele Highway
Hwy. 377 and Hwy 378: Haleakala Highway
Hwy. 380: Kuihelani Highway

From Hana head west on Hwy. 31, which becomes Hwy. 37 after Ulapalakua.

9 Grandma's Coffee House.
I always order the homegrown Haleakala coffee and one of the fresh-baked pastries at this tiny wooden coffeehouse. *At the end of Hwy. 37, Keokea (about 6 miles/9.7km before the Tedeschi Vineyards in Ulupalakua).* ☎ *808/878-2140. $.*

From Grandma's Coffee House, continue on Hwy. 37. Turn right on Hwy. 377 and then right again at Hwy. 378 to the top of Haleakala.

10 ★★★ Haleakala National Park.
Leave Hana early and drive around the Kaupo side of Haleakala (stopping for a mid-morning snack at Grandma's Coffee House, see above), and then up the 10,000-foot (3,048km) dormant volcano, **Haleakala**. Although you won't have time on this trip to hike into the crater, spend an hour wandering around the park. *See p 82 for details.* ☎ *808/572-4400. www.nps.gov/hale. Daily 7am–4pm.*

Retrace your steps back down Hwy. 378, then turn right on Hwy. 377 and right again on Hwy. 37. At the light, turn right on Makawao Avenue and drive into the town of Makawao. To get to Paia from Makawao, head downhill on Baldwin Avenue, which ends in Paia.

11 Makawao. Tour A the old cowboy town, then plan a sunset dinner in B Paia (p 62), before heading back to the airport. *See p 33,* 11 *and* 12 *for more information.*

From Hwy. 36 in Paia, drive to Kahului, turning right on Dairy Road and continuing on to Keolani Place and the airport.

The old cowboy town of Makawao.

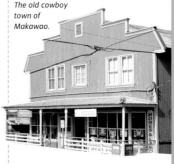

The Best in One Week

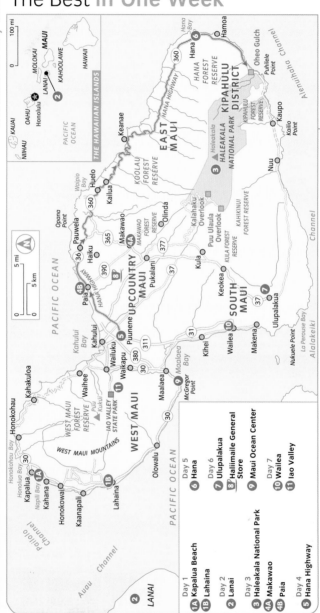

THE HAWAIIAN ISLANDS

Day 1
1A Kapalua Beach
1B Lahaina

Day 2
2 Lanai

Day 3
3 Haleakala National Park
4A Makawao
4B Paia

Day 4
5 Hana Highway

Day 5
6 Hana

Day 6
7 Ulupalakua
8 Haliimaile General Store

Day 7
9 Maui Ocean Center
10 Wailea
11 Iao Valley

Ideally, I recommend you stay at least a week on Maui to take in this sensuous island at a slow, leisurely pace. This week-long itinerary adds a few new favorites to the 3-day tour: sailing to the island of Lanai; seeing the sharks and other ocean creatures at the Maui Ocean Center; and, depending on your preference, a final day on the beach, at a spa, or shopping for souvenirs. To avoid unnecessary driving I'd suggest staying in West Maui (Lahaina/Kaanapali/Kapalua) the first 3 nights, in Hana the next 3 nights, and in South Maui (Kihei/Wailea) on the last night. START: **Kapalua Beach.** **Trip length: 248 miles (399km).**

Travel Tip

West Maui is the area from Lahaina north, including Kaapanali, Honokowai, Kahana, Napili, and Kapalua. South Maui includes Kihei, Wailea, and Makena.

To get to Kapalua Beach from West Maui, drive north on Hwy. 30 to Kapalua. Turn left at the Kapalua Resort sign onto Office Road and follow it to the end. Take a left on Honoapiilai Road, and a right at the beach access sign next-door to the Napili Kai condominium.

1A ★★ Kapalua Beach & 1B Lahaina. For detailed suggestions on how to make the most of your first day, see Day 1 in "The Best in Three Days," p 11.

Go south on Hwy. 30 to Lahaina. Turn right at the light on Dickenson Street. Look for the REPUBLIC PARKING sign on the right. During nonrush hour, allow ½ hour from Kapalua and 15 minutes from Kaanapali.

2 ★★★ Lanai. Get out on the water early with **Trilogy** (p 101), my favorite sailing-snorkeling trip in Hawaii. You'll spend the morning sailing to the island of Lanai, snorkeling, touring the island, and sailing back to Lahaina (breakfast and lunch included). In the afternoon you can go shopping for souvenirs or relax. For dinner, I'd book a table on the ocean at sunset at the **Mala Wailea**

Check your brakes before racing down Haleakala on a bike.

Tedeschi Winery's tasting room.

(p 126), followed by the drama-dance-music show, 'Ulalena (p 146).

Take Hwy. 30 south. Turn right on Hwy. 380, right again on Hwy. 36, then another right on Hwy. 37. Just after Pukalani, turn left on Hwy. 377. Turn left again at the sign to the Haleakala National Park on Hwy. 378 and take it to the top. The summit is 40 to 50 miles (64–80km) from West Maui. Allow at least 2 hours.

❸ ★★★ Haleakala National Park. Head up the 10,000-foot-high (3,048m) dormant volcano, Haleakala. You can hike in the crater (p 87), speed down the mountain on a bicycle (p 95), or simply wander about the park. You don't have to be at the top for sunrise, but I have to tell you—it is a near-religious experience you'll never forget. ☎ *808/572-4400. www. nps .gov/hale. Daily 7am–4pm.*

Retrace your route down the mountain, and turn right at the light on Makawao Avenue. To get to Paia from Makawao, head downhill on Baldwin Avenue, which ends in Paia.

❹A Makawao & ❹B Paia. *See p 33, ⓫ and ⓬.*

To return to West Maui take Hwy. 30 north toward the Kahului Airport and turn left on Dairy Road, which becomes Hwy. 380. Turn left on Hwy. 30 all the way to Lahaina/Kaanapali. The trip is about 30 to 40 miles (48–64km) and takes at least 1 to 1½ hours.

❺ ★★★ Hana Highway. *See p 12, ❺.*

❻ ★★★ Hana. Since you have the entire day to spend, I recommend checking out **Hamoa** or **Red Sand** beaches (see chapter 5); snorkeling or kayaking (rent equipment from **Hana-Maui Sea Sports,** p 104), or touring one of the largest ancient Hawaiian temples in the state, **Piilanihale Heiau** (p 69). Also check out the suggestions on p 12, ❽. Spend another night in Hana.

Get on the road by 10am for Day 6. Head west on Hwy. 360 to Ulupalakua, allowing at least 1 hour driving time. After Kaupo, Hwy 360 becomes Hwy. 31.

❼ Ulupalakua. As you continue driving around the island, make sure to stop at the **Ulupalakua Ranch** and the **Tedeschi Winery** (p 63, ❹) in Ulupalakua. I generally can't resist getting a cup of java at **Grandma's Coffee House;** see p 13, ❾.

After Ulapalakua, Hwy. 31 is called Hwy. 37. Take Hwy. 37 north, then turn right on Hali-imaile Road (just beyond MM 5). The drive takes 30 to 40 minutes.

Heading down the mountain, stop for lunch in the middle of the pine-apple fields at ❽ **Haliimaile General Store.** *See p 124.*

Get back on Hwy. 37, turn right, heading downhill. Turn left at the intersection of Hwy. 36, and left again on Dairy Road, which becomes Hwy. 380. When the road ends, turn left on Hwy. 30; the left turn to Maalaea comes up in less than a mile. The Maui Ocean Center is at the entrance to the village. The drive will take 30 to 40 minutes.

9 Maui Ocean Center. Spend the afternoon checking out the marine life, especially the sharks, in this marvelous aquarium. Since tomorrow's itinerary is in South Maui, Wailea, I'd suggest staying in Wailea tonight. For more information, see p 26, **7**. *Maalaea Harbor Village, 192 Maalaea Rd.* ☎ *808/ 270-7000. www.mauioceancenter. com.*

To get to South Maui from Maalaea, turn right on Hwy. 30, then right on Hwy. 31. To get to Wailea Beach from South Maui (allow 15 min. from the north end of Kihei), take Hwy. 31 south, which ends on Wailea Iki Drive. Turn right on Wailea Iki Drive. At the stop sign (note the Shops at Wailea straight ahead), turn left on Wailea Alanui Road and look for the blue shoreline access sign, which will take you to a public parking lot.

Iao Valley.

Wailea Beach.

10 Wailea. Depending on how much time you have on your final day, you can choose from relaxing on the beach, snorkeling with tropical fish, being pampered in a spa, or shopping. I never pass up an opportunity to go to my favorite beach in South Maui, **Wailea Beach** (p 80), fronting the Four Seasons Maui and the Grand Wailea resorts (you don't have to stay at these resorts to use the beach). Spagoers have a range of terrific spas to choose from (p 36) and shopping aficionados should check out some of my favorite stores at the nearby **Shops at Wailea** (p 140).

To go from Wailea Beach to Iao Valley, head north on Hwy. 31 and turn right on Hwy. 30. In the town of Wailuku, turn left at the light onto Main Street, which becomes Iao Valley Road, and ends at Iao Valley State Park. The 8-mile (13km) trip will take about 30 to 40 minutes.

11 Iao Valley. If you have a late flight, you might want to spend some time in this historic area on your way back to the airport. *See p 60,* **2**.

The Best in Two Weeks

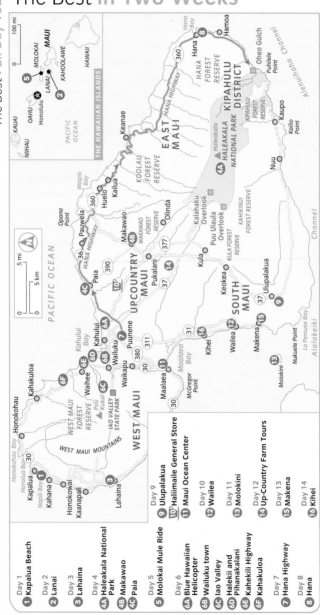

THE HAWAIIAN ISLANDS

Day 1
1 Kapalua Beach

Day 2
2 Lanai

Day 3
3 Lahaina

Day 4
4A Haleakala National Park
4B Makawao
4C Paia

Day 5
5 Molokai Mule Ride

Day 6
6A Blue Hawaiian Helicopter
6B Wailuku town
6C Iao Valley
6D Halekii and Pihanakalani
6E Kahekili Highway
6F Kahakuloa

Day 7
7 Hana Highway

Day 8
8 Hana

Day 9
9 Ulupalakua
10 Haliimaile General Store
11 Maui Ocean Center

Day 10
12 Wailea

Day 11
13 Molokini

Day 12
14 Up-Country Farm Tours

Day 13
15 Makena

Day 14
16 Kihei

Two weeks on Maui separates the visitors from the adventurers and gives you time to really get to know this exotic isle. This tour is similar to the 1-week tour earlier with a few additional stops: flying to Molokai and riding a mule into the dramatic Kalaupapa Peninsula; seeing Maui from a helicopter; driving around the backside of Maui; snorkeling in the old volcanic crater of Molokini; touring Maui's farms; and kayaking off historic Makena. To reduce driving time, plan on spending 6 nights in West Maui, 2 nights in Hana, and 5 nights in South Maui. START: **Kapalua Beach.** End: Kihei. **Trip length: 538 miles (866km).**

1 ★★★ **Kapalua Beach.** *See p 11,* **1**.

2 Lanai. *See p 15,* **2**.

Turn right on Hwy. 30 to Lahaina town.

3 ★★ **Lahaina.** Plan to arrive in this historic town early, before the crowds. I recommend **Lahaina Coolers** (p 125) for a big breakfast, then put on your walking shoes and take the self-guided **historic walking tour** of the old town (p 50), do some browsing in the quaint stores (p 132), watch the surfers skim the waves in front of the library, and pop over to Kaanapali to the **Whale Center of the Pacific** (p 43).

Take Hwy. 30 south. Turn right on Hwy. 380, right again on Hwy. 36, then another right on Hwy. 37. Just after Pukalani, turn left on Hwy. 377. Turn right at the sign to the Haleakala National Park on Hwy. 378 and take it to the top. The summit is 40 to 50 miles (64–80km) from West Maui. Allow at least 2 hours.

4 ★★★ **Haleakala National Park.** For details on exploring this volcano, plus the rural towns of **4A Makawao** and **4B Paia,** see p 33, **11** and **12**.

To take the ferry to Molokai from Lahaina Harbor, take Hwy. 30 south to Lahaina. At the light at Dickenson Street, turn left. Park and walk toward the ocean to Front Street. After the library, turn toward the ocean to the harbor.

Haleakala's crater.

Riding a mule on Molokai.

5 ★★★ **Molokai Mule Ride.** For an unforgettable all-day adventure on the "Friendly Isle" take a mule ride into the **Kalaupapa Peninsula.** Starting at the top of the nearly perpendicular ridge (1,600-ft./488km high), Buzzy Sproat's surefooted mules step down the narrow, muddy 3-mile (4.8km) trail daily, rain or shine, pausing often on the 26 switchbacks to calculate their next move—and always, it seems to me, veering a little too close to the edge. Each switchback is numbered; by the time you get to number four, you'll catch your breath, put the mule on cruise control, and begin to enjoy Hawaii's most awesome trail ride. With a minimum of two people, you can also arrange to fly over for the day for an additional fee. 🕐 *7.5 hr. 100 Kalae Hwy., Ste. 104, on Hwy. 470, 5 miles (8km) north of Hwy. 460.* ☎ *800/567-7550. www.muleride. com. Tours are offered daily starting at 8am. $165 per person. Riders must be at least 16 years old and physically fit.*

To get to the Heliport, head out on Hwy. 30, turn right on Hwy. 380, which becomes Dairy Road. Turn right at the intersection of Hwy. 37. You will circle around the airport runway. Make a left on Leleipio Place.

Avoiding Rush Hour

Set out early or late to avoid Maui's rush hour, which lasts from 7 to 9am and from 4 to 6pm. Roads can be packed bumper-to-bumper—not a fun way to spend your vacation!

6 ★★★ **See Maui from above in a helicopter.** Flying over Maui in a helicopter will give you an entirely different perspective of the island, and of all the helicopter companies, I think **Blue Hawaiian Helicopter** (p 95) offers the most comfortable, informative, and fun tours. After your flight, head to Wailuku Town by retracing your steps back to Hwy. 37. Continue on Hwy. 37 where it merges with Hwy. 36. Follow Hwy. 36 until it merges with Hwy. 32 (Kaahumanu Ave.), which will take you into Wailuku (the street name changes to Main St. in Wailuku). Take some time to explore the old town of **6A** **Wailuku** (see the walking tour on p 42), wandering through the shops and stopping at the Bailey House on West Main Street. Continue on Main Street,

Viewing Maui from a helicopter.

Molokini's distinctive crescent is the perfect haven for colorful, tropical fish.

which becomes Iao Valley Road, to the end where you will be in 6B **Iao Valley** (p 60). From here, retrace your route back to Main Street. Make a left on Market Street, then a right on Mill Street, which ends at Lower Main Street, turn left and then left again onto Waiheu Beach Road (Hwy. 340). Go left on Kuhio Place and then take your first left on Hea Place. At the end of the street are the ancient temples of 6C **Halekii** and **Pihanakalani.** If you aren't too tired, return to West Maui via the 6D **Kahekili Highway.** Get here by retracing your route back to Waiheu Beach Road (Hwy. 340) and turning left. When the road ends, make a right on Kahekili Highway (Hwy. 340), stopping to see the ancient Hawaiian village of 6E **Kahakuloa** (12 miles/19km down the windy road) and then continue on to Lahaina, another 21 miles (34km) away. For more on the temples, Kahekili Highway, and Kahakuloa, see the "Maui's History & Culture" tour, p 42.

To reach Hana Highway from Lahaina/Kaanapali, take Hwy. 30 south to Hwy. 380 and turn right (east). In Kahului Hwy. 380 becomes Dairy Road. Turn right (east) on Hwy. 36.

Travel Tip

The next leg of your trip will follow the recommendations in "The Best in One Week." Start with p 16, 5 (Hana Hwy.) and follow the directions and recommendations through p 17, 10 (Wailea).

7 **Hana Highway.** *See p 12,* 5.

8 ★★★ **Hana.** *See p 16,* 6.

9 **Ulupalakua.** *See p 16,* 7.

10 **Haliimaile General Store.** *See p 16,* 8.

11 **Maui Ocean Center.** *See p 17,* 9.

To reach Wailea, see the directions on p 17.

12 **Wailea.** A great place to relax on the beach, get pampered at a spa or go shopping. *See p 17,* 10.

The boat trip to Molokini departs from Maalaea Harbor. Travel on Hwy. 30 north, turn left on Hwy. 30. The left-turn exit to Maalaea comes up within a mile.

13 ★★★ **Molokini.** Take a day to see the fish inside the Molokini

Kayaking in La Pérouse Bay near the `Ahihi-Kina`u Natural Area Reserve.

Crater. Go in the morning before the wind comes up. If it's whale season and you're lucky, you may spot whales on the way over or back. I recommend taking one of **Trilogy's** tours (p 101).

Depending on traffic, allow at least an hour to drive from South Maui to the Ali'i Kula Lavender Farm. Take Hwy. 31 north and turn right onto Hwy. 311. At the light on Hwy. 380, turn right on Dairy Road. Turn right onto Hwy. 37, and follow it up the mountain to Kula. Take the second left after Rice Park onto Kekauliki Avenue. Drive about ¼ mile (.4km), rounding a bend, taking a quick right up Waipoli Road. From the lavender farm to the Surfing Goat Dairy, retrace your route to the Kula Highway. About 3 miles (4.8km) along the Kula Highway, make a left down Omaopio Road. In about 3 miles (4.8km) you'll see the farm sign on the left.

🄮 **Upcountry farm tours.** Plan at least one off-the-beaten-path tour while you're on Maui. For a really exotic experience, plus terrific food, take the **Combo Tour of the Ali'i Kula Lavender Farm** (p 32, 🄌), which includes a walking tour of the farm and a lunch basket made with lavender products. Cheese aficionados will love the **Surfing Goat Dairy Tour** (p 39, 🄌) and the sampling of their cheeses.

To get to Makena Beach on Day 13, take Hwy. 31 south, which ends at Wailea Ike Drive. Turn left at the intersection onto Wailea Alanui Road, which becomes Makean Alanui Road. Turn right on Makena Road to Makena Bay.

From there to La Pérouse Bay continue on Makena Road until it ends, then take off on foot for a couple of miles to reach the bay.

🄯 **Makena.** Kayaking is so easy here that you'll be paddling away within a few minutes of taking a lesson. The water is calm and clear enough that you can see the fish, and you are protected from the wind (see "Kayak Tours," p 104). After a couple of hours of kayaking and snorkeling, stop for a picnic lunch at **Makena Landing,** then explore this area. If you have some energy to spare, hike over to **La Pérouse Bay,** along the rugged shoreline, and see the `Ahihi-Kina`u Natural Area Reserve (p 99).

Head north on South Kihei Road.

🄰 **Kihei.** After 13 days of exploring Maui, spend your last day doing whatever you love best, whether it's beach hopping the 5 miles (8km) of white-sand beaches that line the town of Kihei (p 57), beachcombing, snorkeling, or shopping. Pick up a lei at the Kmart on Dairy Road near the airport before you fly out so you will have a little bit of Maui with you as you say aloha. ●

One of Kihei's beaches.

Maui **with** Kids

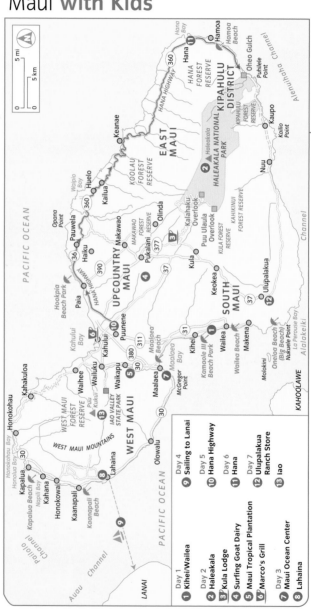

0 5 mi
0 5 km

LANAI

Auau Channel

PACIFIC OCEAN

Pailolo Channel

Kahakuloa

Honokohau

Honokohau Bay
Honolua Bay
Napili Bay
Kapalua
Kapalua Beach
Kahana
Honokowai
Kaanapali
Kaanapali Beach

WEST MAUI

WEST MAUI MOUNTAINS

WEST MAUI
FOREST
RESERVE

Puu
Kukui

IAO VALLEY
STATE PARK

Lahaina

Olowalu

Kahakuloa

Waihee
Waikapu
Wailuku

Puunene

Kahului
Kahului Bay

PACIFIC OCEAN

Hookipa
Beach Park

Paia

Haiku

Pauwela

Opana
Point

Waipio
Bay

Huelo

Kailua

Keanae

Hana
Bay

Hamoa
Hamoa
Beach

Oheo Gulch
Puhiele
Point

Alenuihaha Channel

KIPAHULU
DISTRICT

KIPAHULU
FOREST
RESERVE

Kaupo

Kailio
Point

Nuu

HANA
FOREST
RESERVE

HALEAKALA NATIONAL
PARK

Haleakala

KAHIKINUI
FOREST RESERVE

KULA FOREST
RESERVE

Kalahaku
Overlook

Puu Ulaula
Overlook

EAST MAUI

KOOLAU
FOREST
RESERVE

MAKAWAO
FOREST
RESERVE

Makawao
Olinda

Pukalani

Kula

Keokea

Ulupalakua

SOUTH MAUI

Makena

Molokini

Oneloa Beach
(Big Beach)
Nukuele Point
La Perouse Bay

Alalakeiki

KAHOOLAWE

Wailea
Wailea Beach
Kamaole III
Beach Park
Kihei

Maalaea
Maalaea Bay

McGregor
Point

Puunene

UPCOUNTRY MAUI

HANA HIGHWAY

HANA HIGHWAY

Channel

Day 1
❶ Kihei/Wailea

Day 2
❷ Haleakala
③ Kula Lodge
❹ Surfing Goat Dairy
❺ Maui Tropical Plantation
⑥ Marco's Grill

Day 3
❼ Maui Ocean Center
❽ Lahaina

Day 4
❾ Sailing to Lanai

Day 5
❿ Hana Highway

Day 6
⓫ Hana

Day 7
⓬ Ulupalakua
Ranch Store
⓭ Iao

Previous page: Maui's pineapple fields.

Your itinerary is going to depend on the ages of your kids. The number-one rule is *don't plan too much,* especially with young children, who will be fighting jet lag, trying to get adjusted to a new bed (and most likely new food), and may be hyped up to the point of exhaustion. The 7-day itinerary below is a guide to the various family-friendly activities available on Maui; I'd suggest staying in South Maui (Kihei or Wailea) for the first 2 nights, then moving to West Maui (Lahaina or Kaanapali) for the next 2 nights, and then to Hana for your last 2 nights. START: **Kihei/Wailea. Trip length: 7 days and 295 miles (475km).**

Travel Tip

See chapter 7 for hotel recommendations and chapter 8 for detailed reviews of the restaurants mentioned in this chapter.

① **Kihei/Wailea.** In my experience, the first thing kids want to do is hit the water. A great, safe beach to start with is **Wailea** (p 80), fronting the Four Seasons and the Grand Wailea resorts. If you have young kids who are not used to the waves, you might consider taking them to the swimming pool at your hotel. They'll be happy playing in the water, and you won't have to introduce them to ocean safety after that long plane ride. If this is your first day in Maui, you'll probably want an early dinner, with food your kids are used to. My pick of family-friendly eateries in Kihei are either **Shaka Sandwich & Pizza** (p 128) or **Stella Blues Cafe** (p 128). Get to bed early.

Allow 2 to 2½ hours to reach the Haleakala summit from South Maui. Go north on Hwy. 31 to Hwy. 311, then go right on Hwy. 36 and right again on Hwy. 37. Then take Hwy. 377 to Hwy. 378.

② **★★★ Haleakala.** Your family will probably be up early, so take advantage and head up to the 10,000-foot (3,048m) dormant volcano Haleakala. Depending on the

After a long plane ride, the beach is a great first stop for kids and adults.

age of your children, you can either hike in the crater, speed down the mountain on a bicycle, or just wander about the park. See chapter 6 for details. ☎ *808/572-4400. www. nps.gov/hale. Daily 7am–4pm.*

③ **Kula Lodge.** Depending on how hungry your kids are, I'd suggest taking them to breakfast here either on the way to or from Haleakala. *Haleakala Hwy. (Hwy. 377).* ☎ *808/878-2517. $$.*

From the summit, allow 45 minutes to retrace Hwy. 378 to Hwy.

The train ride through Maui Tropical Plantation.

377, to Hwy. 37 and turn left onto Omaopio Road. Look for the SURFING GOAT DAIRY sign on the left about 2 miles (3.2km) down.

❹ Surfing Goat Dairy. The kids (yours) will love petting and playing with the other kids (the goat variety). Don't leave without sampling the selection of cheeses. For more information, see p 39.

Continue down the mountain on Omaopio Road, which after MM 5 joins Pulehu Road (Hwy. 370). When the road ends, turn left on Hwy. 36 and left on Kaahumanu Avenue continuing through Kahului and Wailuku. Kaahumanu Avenue becomes Main Street in Wailuku. At the stop light of Main and High streets, turn left on High Street (Hwy. 30).Just after the town of Waikapu, about a ½ mile (.8km) after MM 2, look for the sign on the right. The trip will take you about 35 to 45 minutes.

❺ Maui Tropical Plantation. This plantation in Waikapu offers a 40-minute tram ride through exotic flora and fruit that will amuse even jaded teenagers. See p 39.

Turn left out of the Maui Tropical Plantation onto Hwy. 30. Turn right on Waiko Road (Hwy. 305) and follow it until it ends. Make a left on Hwy. 380, which becomes Dairy Road after a couple of miles. Look for Marco's Grill and Deli on the left.

🍴 Marco's Grill and Deli. Tonight I recommend another early dinner; this Kahului restaurant is popular for its Italian fare, and offers a menu sure to please those hard-to-please kids.

Take Hwy. 31 north and go left on Hwy. 30 to Maalaea. Depending on the location of your accommodations, allow about 30 minutes.

❼ ★★★ Maui Ocean Center. After a lazy breakfast, wander over here so your kids can see the fabulous underwater world of sharks, stingrays, and starfish, without having to get wet. Plan to spend the morning immersed in the 5-acre (2ha) oceanarium, then have lunch at the center's **Reef Café.** ⏱ *2 to 3 hr. Maalaea Harbor Village, 192 Maalaea Rd., Maalaea.* ☎ *808/270-7000. www.mauioceancenter.com. Daily 9am–5pm.*

Head north on Hwy. 30 to Lahaina. The drive takes about 20 to 30 minutes.

Maui Ocean Center.

8 Lahaina. In Lahaina you can take the kids underwater in a Jules Verne–type fantasy, the **Atlantis Submarine** (658 Front St.; ☎ **800/ 548-6262** or 808/667-7816; www. goatlantis.com). You'll plunge 100 feet (30m) under the sea in a state-of-the-art, high-tech submarine and meet swarms of vibrant tropical fish up close and personal as they flutter through the deep blue waters. Atlantis offers trips out of Lahaina Harbor every hour on the hour from 9am to 2pm. The fare is $89 for adults and $45 for children 11 and under (children must be at least 3 ft./.9m tall). Book on the website and save 10%. Allow 2 hours for this underwater adventure. Younger kids may prefer the **Lahaina–Kaanapali Sugar Cane Train** (☎ **808/661-0089**; www.sugarcanetrain.com). Kids of all ages will enjoy hitting one of the terrific **beaches** on West Maui (see chapter 5) and maybe renting some snorkel equipment. Book ahead for the **Old Lahaina Luau** (p 124) in the evening. Plan to spend the night in Lahaina.

In Lahaina, turn toward the ocean at the light on Dickenson Street. Look for the REPUBLIC PARKING sign, on the right.

The Atlantis Submarine.

9 ★★★ Sailing to Lanai. Trilogy (p 101) offers the best sailing-snorkeling trip in Hawaii, so don't miss it. In the afternoon, wander around Lahaina (p 50) and hit a few kid-friendly highlights, including the giant banyan tree, the Old Lahaina Courthouse, and the Old Prison. In the evening, older kids may be interested in checking out the night skies with the Hyatt Regency Maui Resort's Tour of the Stars, complete with a computer-driven telescope. Contact the Hyatt Regency Maui (☎ 800/233-1234 or 808/661-1234; www.maui.hyatt.com) to book.

A Great Way to Spend a Rainy Day

If it rains during your vacation, take the kids to the Kapalua Resort **Hawaiian Cultural Art's Kukui Room** (☎ 800/KAPALUA [527-2582] or 808/669-5433; www.kapalua.com/recreation/hawaiian_culture), located in the resort's Honolua Village Center. The Hawaiian cultural advisor for Kapalua leads wonderful classes and demonstrations for the entire family in everything from lei making to hula dancing, even how to identify Hawaiian native plants. The school features local and visiting instructors, and is open Monday, Wednesday, and Friday for people of all ages and skill levels. Call to see what's scheduled.

Go south on Hwy. 30, right on Hwy. 380, and right on Hwy. 36 to Hana. With stops, this drive can take up to a whole day.

⑩ ★★★ **Hana Highway.** Pack a lunch and spend the day driving the unforgettable Hana Highway. Pull over often and let the kids get out to take photos, smell the flowers, and jump in the mountain-stream pools. Plan to spend at least 2 nights in Hana. See p 64.

⑪ ★★★ **Hana.** Hana is an entire day in paradise, with so many things to do. Take an early-morning hike along the black sands of **Waianapanapa State Park,** then explore

The Road to Hana features spectacular waterfalls.

the tiny town of Hana. Make sure you see the **Hana Cultural Center and Museum,** the **Hasagawa General Store,** and the **Hana Coast Gallery.** Get a picnic lunch and drive out to the **Kipihulu end of Haleakala National Park at Oheo Gulch.** Hike to the waterfalls, swim in the pools, take lots of photos. Splurge on dinner and eat at the dining room in the **Hotel Hana-Maui** (p 113). See p 68 for a detailed tour of Hana.

Continue past Hana on Hwy. 360, which becomes Hwy. 31 at Kaupo to Ulupalakua. Allow 45 minutes to an hour.

⑫ **Ulupalakua Ranch Store.** By the time you get to the upcountry town of Ulupalakua, the kids will be restless. This eclectic general store, which dates back to 1849, is a good place for you all to stretch your legs—you can also grab lunch at the small deli inside. See p 63.

Go north on Hwy. 37 and left on Hwy. 36 through Kahului and Wailuku. Continue straight at the light at Main Street/Hwy. 30 and follow Iao Valley Road to its end. The drive will take 45 to 60 minutes.

⑬ **Iao.** If you have some time before your flight home, I'd recommend spending the afternoon at the **Hawaii Nature Center** (875 Iao Valley Rd.; ☎ 808/244-6500; www.hawaiinaturecenter.org), which has some 30 interactive exhibits on nature. Don't miss the Rainforest Walk, a moderate loop trail through the ancient footpaths in **Iao Valley** (p 60, ②). This guided walk includes commentary on native Hawaiian plants, the remains of ancient habitation, and stories of old Hawaii.

Hiking in Waianapanapa State Park.

Family-Friendly Events

Your trip may be a little more enjoyable with the added attraction of attending a celebration, festival, or party on Maui. Check out the following events:

- **Chinese New Year,** Lahaina (☎ 888/310-1117). **This holiday can fall in either January or February.** February 14, 2010, starts the year of the tiger and February 3, 2011, starts the year of the rabbit. Lahaina rolls out the red carpet with a traditional lion dance, accompanied by fireworks, food booths, and a host of activities.

- **Whale Day Celebration,** Kalama Park, Kihei (☎ 808/249-8811; www.visitmaui.com). In early to mid-February, this daylong celebration features a parade of whales, entertainment, a crafts fair, games, and food.

- **Ocean Arts Festival,** Lahaina (☎ 888/310-1117; www.visit lahaina.com). Kids will love this mid-March event with marine-related activities, games, and a touch-pool exhibit.

- **Annual Lei Day Celebration,** islandwide (☎ 808/875-4100; www.visitmaui.com). May Day is Lei Day in Hawaii, celebrated with lei-making contests, pageantry, arts and crafts, and concerts.

- **King Kamehameha Celebration,** islandwide (☎ 888/310-1117; www.visitlahaina.com). June 10 is a state holiday with a massive floral parade, *hoolaulea* (party), and much more.

- **Fourth of July,** Lahaina (☎ 888/310-1117; www.visitlahaina.com). Lahaina holds an old-fashioned Independence Day celebration with fireworks. Kaanapali (☎ 808/661-3271) puts on a grand-old celebration with live music, children's activities, and fireworks.

- **Maui County Fair,** War Memorial Complex, Wailuku (☎ 800/525-MAUI [6284]; www.calendarmaui.com). At the end of September, this traditional county fair features a parade, amusement rides, live entertainment, and exhibits.

Romantic Maui

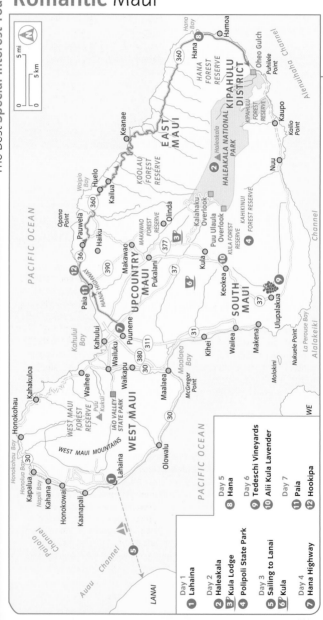

PACIFIC OCEAN

Hana Bay

Hamoa

HANA FOREST RESERVE

KIPAHULU DISTRICT

Oheo Gulch

Puhilele Point

KIPAHULU FOREST RESERVE

Kaupo

Kailio Point

Alenuihaha Channel

360

Hana

EAST MAUI

Keanae

Haleakala

HALEAKALA NATIONAL PARK

HANA FOREST RESERVE

KOOLAU FOREST RESERVE

Kalahaku Overlook

Puu Ulaula Overlook

KAHIKINUI FOREST RESERVE

Nuu

Channel

Waipio Bay

Opana Point

Huelo

Kailua

360

Haiku

Pauwela

36

Olinda

MAKAWAO FOREST RESERVE

Makawao

377

Pukalani

37

Kula

KULA FOREST RESERVE

Keokea

37

Ulupalakua

SOUTH MAUI

La Perouse Bay

Nukuele Point

Alalakeiki

Kahului Bay

HANA HIGHWAY

390

Paia

UPCOUNTRY MAUI

Puunene

Kahului

Wailuku

Waikapu

Waihee

Maalaea

311

380

30

Kihei

Wailea

Makena

Molokini

McGregor Point

Maalaea Bay

WEST MAUI FOREST RESERVE

Puu Kukui

IAO VALLEY STATE PARK

WEST MAUI MOUNTAINS

WEST MAUI

30

Olowalu

Lahaina

PACIFIC OCEAN

Kahakuloa

Honokohau

Honokohau Bay

Honolua Bay

Napili Bay

Kapalua

30

Kahana

Honokowai

Kaanapali

Pailolo Channel

Auau Channel

LANAI

WE

0   5 mi
0   5 km

Day 1
1 Lahaina

Day 2
2 Haleakala
3 Kula Lodge
4 Polipoli State Park

Day 3
5 Sailing to Lanai
6 Kula

Day 4
7 Hana Highway

Day 5
8 Hana

Day 6
9 Tedeschi Vineyards
10 Alii Kula Lavender

Day 7
11 Paia
12 Hookipa

Maui's sensual side makes it the perfect place to fall in love. The smell of flowers in the air, the sound of the waves rolling in, and the island's exotic beauty all beckon lovers. If you're discovering Maui as a twosome, I suggest spending the first 3 nights in Lahaina, the next 2 in Hana, and your last night in the upcountry area. START: **Lahaina. Trip length: 7 days and 333 miles (536km).**

1 Lahaina. Don't leave the Kahului Airport without giving your sweetie a sweet-smelling flower lei. Book my favorite Hawaii experience, the **Old Lahaina Luau** (p 124), where the two of you can watch the sunset while enjoying a mai tai and a meal.

Allow 2 hours to drive to the summit of Haleakala. Head south on Hwy. 30, then go right on Hwy. 380, right on Hwy. 36, and right again on Hwy. 37. Then follow Hwy. 377 to Hwy. 378.

2 Haleakala. If you've just arrived and are still on mainland time, make the most of it and get up early to drive to Haleakala National Park in time for the sunrise on the summit of this dormant volcano. The two of you, wrapped in a blanket (it's cold at 10,000 ft./3,048m), watching the stars slowly fade and the dim rays of dawn appear, will become one of your fondest memories. See p 82.

A selection of sweet-smelling flower leis.

Stop at **3 Kula Lodge** for a big breakfast overlooking the isthmus of Maui. Get a takeout picnic lunch before you leave. See p 125. *$$.*

Head down Hwy. 378, then take a left on Hwy. 377 and go left on Waipoli Road to the end. To return to Lahaina, retrace back, left on Hwy. 377, right on Hwy. 30, and return to Lahaina.

4 Polipoli State Park. In Polipoli you can walk in total silence (except for the sounds of the native birds) among the pine, redwood, and eucalyptus trees. You probably won't see another soul in this 21,000-acre (8,498ha) forest reserve. Have a picnic, take a nap, and return to Lahaina for another sunset dinner, this one at the **Mala Wharf.** See p 88.

In Lahaina, turn toward the ocean at the light on Dickenson Street. Look for the sign REPUBLIC PARKING, on the right side of the street.

5 ★★★ Sailing to Lanai. Nothing is more romantic than the wind kissing your face and the sun warming your skin as the two of you sail offshore to Lanai with **Trilogy** (p 101), my favorite sailing company. On the half-day excursion the crew hands you hot cinnamon rolls and coffee as soon as you step on board, and after the 9-mile (14km) trip to Lanai, there is an island excursion and a barbecue lunch.

Drive south on Hwy. 30, go right on Hwy. 380, right on Hwy. 36, and right again on Hwy. 37 to

The Road to Hana.

Rice park. Allow about an hour from Lahaina to Kula.

Gather up provisions (I like **Moana Bakery & Café;** see p 127) and drive up to Harold W. Rice Memorial Park for a picnic dinner in 6 **Kula** to see the sunset. For a truly magical evening, linger over a bottle of wine or dessert until the stars come out.

From Lahaina, go south on Hwy. 30, turn right on Hwy. 380, then turn right on Hwy. 36 toward Hana. With stops, this drive will take a whole day.

7 **Hana Highway.** Bring your swimsuit, put the top down, and turn the radio up—plan on spending the entire day cruising Maui's most famous curvy road. Stop at waterfalls, go for a swim in tranquil pools, have a picnic, and enjoy every spontaneous moment. See p 64.

8 **Hana.** Lush, tropical Hana is the perfect place for romance and it's well worth spending a couple of nights here. If you're ready for some

relaxing beach time, you can choose the fiery red beach at **Red Sand Beach** (p 79), the perfect crescent white-sand bay at **Hamoa Beach** (p 76), or the freshwater pools at **Oheo Gulch,** where you can sit and soak while watching the waves rolling ashore. Around sunset, walk the ancient Hawaii trail in **Waianapanapa State Park.** For more detailed information on Hana's sights, see the tour on p 68.

Continue past Hana on Hwy. 360, which becomes Hwy. 31 at Kaupo, to Ulupalakua. Allow 45 minutes to an hour.

9 **Tedeschi Vineyards.** Get a picnic lunch before you leave Hana and drive the "backside" around Maui past Kaupo to the winery. After sampling a few of Maui's wines, select a bottle and have your picnic lunch on the grounds of the old estate. See p 40.

Head north on Hwy. 37, to a right on Hwy. 377 for about a quarter of a mile. Once you've rounded the bend, take a quick right up Waipoli Road.

10 **Ali'i Kula Lavender.** In the upcountry Kula region, stop at this lavender farm to pick up lavender bubble bath and a lavender candle. Plan to spend your final night soaking in a romantic hot bath in Maui's upcountry. *1100 Waipoli Rd. Kula.* ☎ *808/878-3004. www.alii kulalavender. com. Daily 9am–4pm.*

Splitting a bottle of wine at Tedeschi Vineyards is a wonderful way to while away an afternoon.

Retrace your steps to Hwy. 37, take a right at the light on Makawao Road, and at the stop sign in Makawao town go left down Baldwin Avenue to the end.

⓫ **Paia.** On your last day, drive to Paia and have breakfast at my favorite cafe, **Moana Bakery & Café** (p 127). Afterward poke around the shops in this tiny town. See chapter 9.

Continue east on Hwy. 36.

⓬ **Hookipa.** Here you can watch the surfers and windsurfers as you feel the warm wind caress your

Windsurfer on Hookipa.

face. This is a great spot for a photo op with that glorious ocean as a backdrop. See p 76.

Getting Maui'd

Maui is a great place for a wedding. Not only does the entire island exude romance and natural beauty, but after the ceremony, you're also only a few steps away from the perfect honeymoon.

Dozens of companies can help you organize an unforgettable wedding. The easiest option is to let someone at the resort or hotel where you'll be staying handle it. Most Maui resorts and hotels have wedding coordinators who can plan everything from a simple (relatively) low-cost wedding to an extravaganza that people will talk about for years. Remember that resorts can be pricey—be frank with your wedding coordinator if you want to keep costs down.

You can also plan your own island wedding, even from afar, without spending a fortune. For a marriage license, contact the **Marriage License Office** in the State Department of Health Building (54 S. High St., Wailuku, HI 96793; ☎ 808/984-8210; www.state.hi.us/doh/records/vr_marri.html). It is open Monday through Friday from 8am to 4pm. The staff will mail you a brochure called *Getting Married* and direct you to the marriage-licensing agent closest to where you'll be staying on Maui. Once on Maui the prospective bride and groom must go together to the marriage-licensing agent to get a license. A license costs $60 and is good for 30 days.

The Wailea Resort's wedding chapel.

The Best Special-Interest Tours

Relax & Rejuvenate on Maui

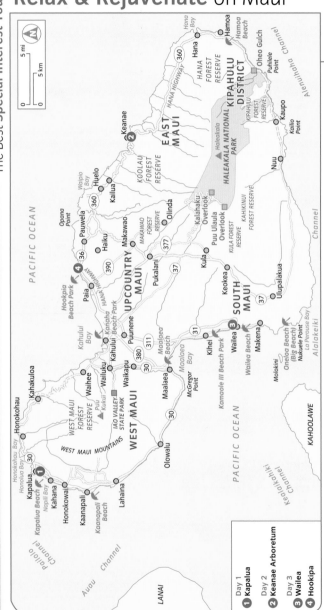

5 mi
0   5 km

Hana Bay
Hamoa
Hamoa Beach
360
HANA HIGHWAY
Hana
HANA FOREST RESERVE
KIPAHULU DISTRICT
Oheo Gulch
Puhilele Point
Alenuihaha Channel
Keanae
2
EAST MAUI
Haleakala
HALEAKALA NATIONAL PARK
KIPAHULU FOREST RESERVE
Kaupo
Kailio Point
KOOLAU FOREST RESERVE
Waipio Bay
Huelo
360
Kailua
Kalahaku Overlook
Olinda
Puu Ulaula Overlook
KAHIKINUI FOREST RESERVE
Opana Point
Pauwela
377
MAKAWAO FOREST RESERVE
Makawao
KULA FOREST RESERVE
PACIFIC OCEAN
Haiku
Pukalani
Kula
36
UPCOUNTRY MAUI
37
Nuu
Channel
Hookipa Beach Park
4
390
HANA HIGHWAY
Paia
Keokea
Ulupalakua
Kahului Beach Park
Kahului Bay
Kahului
Puunene
Kanaha Beach Park
311
31
SOUTH MAUI
37
Wailea
3
Kahakuloa
Waihee
Wailuku
380
Waikapu
30
Maalaea Beach
Maalaea Bay
Kihei
Wailea Beach
Makena
Molokini
Oneloa Beach (Big Beach)
Nukule Point
La Perouse Bay
Alalakeiki
Honokohau
Honokohau Bay
Honolua Bay
WEST MAUI FOREST RESERVE
Puu Kukui
IAO VALLEY STATE PARK
WEST MAUI MOUNTAINS
WEST MAUI
Maalaea
McGregor Point
Kamaole III Beach Park
Kapalua
30
1
Kapalua Beach
Napili Bay
Kahana
Honokowai
Kaanapali
Kaanapali Beach
Lahaina
30
Olowalu
PACIFIC OCEAN
KAHOOLAWE
Keolaikahiki Channel
Pailolo Channel
Auau Channel
LANAI

Day 1
1 Kapalua
Day 2
2 Keanae Arboretum
Day 3
3 Wailea
4 Hookipa

Maui's beautiful weather, unspoiled beaches, lush tropical vegetation, and invigorating tradewinds are just the recipe to soothe your body, mind, and spirit. Below are my favorite ways to relax over a 3-day weekend. START: **Kapalua. Trip length: 3 days and 195 miles (314km).**

❶ Kapalua. Start the day off by booking a massage on the beach at the **Ritz-Carlton Kapalua** (p 116). The spa itself is welcoming and wonderful, but I love the smell of salt in the air and feeling the wind gently caressing my hair while experiencing a true Hawaiian massage. Grab a picnic lunch at the **Honolua Store** (p 138) and walk down to **D. T. Fleming Beach** (p 76) and plan to spend the afternoon just reading a good book or floating in the warm, tropical waters. For a soothing, relaxing dinner, try the **Pineapple Grill Kapalua** (p 127).

Head south on Hwy. 30 and go left on Hwy. 380. Go right on Hwy. 30, which becomes Hwy. 360. The rainforest is after MM 16, just past the Keanae YMCA Camp and before the turn off to the Keanae Peninsula. Allow 2 to 3 hours for the 80-mile (129km) trip.

❷ Keanae Arboretum. This easy 2-mile (3.2km) stroll through a rainforest is a wonderful way to relax and commune with nature. (Excepting mosquitoes and rain—bring repellant and rain gear to ward them off.) I'd allow at least 2 hours here, longer if you bring your swimsuit and plunge into my

favorite swimming hole near the end of the trail. Park at the Keanae Arboretum and pass through the turnstile. You start off on a flat trail where you can look around at the plants which have been introduced to Hawaii (all with identification tags). At the end of this section is a taro patch, with a half-dozen different varieties of this staple crop. You can also follow a 1-mile (1.6km) trail where you can smell the fragrances of the tropical jungle, and listen to the sounds of the birds and the nearby stream. The trail crisscrosses the stream through the forest, but I prefer to cool off at the pond, just to the left of the first stream crossing. Plan to spend the night in Hana (about 40 min. down the highway) at the **Hotel Hana-Maui** (p 113).

Head south on Hwy. 360, which becomes Hwy. 31 after Kaupo and then Hwy 37 after Ulupalakua. Continue on Hwy. 37 at Pukalani. Go left on Hwy. 36, left on Hansen Road, left on Hwy. 311, and left again on Hwy. 31. When Hwy. 31 ends, take a right onto Wailea Iki Drive. Then go left on Wailea Alanui Drive. Allow 3 to 4 hours for the 65-mile (105km) trip.

Relax, Breathe Deep & Say "Sp-Ahh"

Hawaii's spas are airy, open facilities that embrace the tropics. Here are your best options on Maui:

- **Spa Grande at the Grand Wailea Resort** (☎ 800/888-6100 or 808/875-1234; www.grandwailea.com): This is Hawaii's biggest spa, combining the finest Eastern traditions (a full Japanese-style traditional bath and various exotic treatments from India), and the lure of the islands (tropical foliage, ancient Hawaiian treatments, and island products). It has everything from a top fitness center to a menu of classes.

- **Spa Kea Lani at the Fairmont Kea Lani Maui** (☎ 800/659-4100 or 808/875-4100; www.fairmont.com/kealani): This intimate, Art Deco boutique spa is the place for personal, private attention. The fitness center next door is open 24 hours (a rarity in Hawaiian resorts) with a personal trainer on duty.

- **Spa Moana at the Hyatt Regency Maui Resort & Spa** (☎ 800/233-1234 or 808/661-1234; www.maui.hyatt.com): This facility offers an open-air exercise lanai, wet-treatment rooms, massage rooms, a relaxation lounge, sauna and steam rooms, a Roman pool illuminated by overhead skylights, and a duet treatment suite for couples.

- **Spa at Ritz-Carlton Kapalua** (☎ 800/262-8440 or 808/669-6200; www.ritzcarlton.com): Book a massage at the newly opened 17,500-square-foot (1,626-sq.-m), Waihua Spa. Waihua translates as "healing waters." The treatments here are based on ancient Hawaiian techniques and theories on healing.

- **The Spa at the Four Seasons Resort Maui at Wailea** (☎ 800/334-MAUI [6284] or 808/874-8000; www.fourseasons.com/maui): Imagine the sounds of the waves rolling on Wailea Beach as you are soothingly massaged in the privacy of your cabana, tucked into the beachside foliage. This is the place to come to be absolutely spoiled.

Enjoying a massage at the Fairmont.

A painted eucalyptus tree with a philodendron leaf at the Keanae Arboretum.

Lani Maui. See the box on p 36 for details. After your treatment, lunch at **Longhi's** (p 126).

From Wailea take Hwy. 31 north, go right on Hwy. 311 and right again on Hwy. 36 to Hookipa. Allow 40 to 45 minutes driving time.

④ **Hookipa.** In the afternoon sit on the bluff overlooking this windsurfing beach (p 76) and watch the colorful sailboarders lift into the air and twirl like butterflies. At sunset, simply go next door for a fresh fish dinner at **Mama's Fish House** (p 126).

③ **Wailea.** This is the holy land of spas. I'd book one of the following: a Seashell Massage (using seashells in combination with the Hawaiian *lomi lomi* massage for relief of tense muscles, sore joints, and stressed emotions) at the **Spa Grande at the Grand Wailea Resort;** the Signature Treatment (4 diverse techniques, including a peppermint scrub, warm herbal wrap, massage medley, finishing with a soothing scalp treatment) at **the Spa at the Four Seasons Resort Maui;** or the Blissful Spa Experience (*gotu kola, noni,* and kava scrub, then an aroma tropical bath, followed by a Hawaiian *lomi lomi* massage) at the **Spa Kea Lani at the Fairmont Kea

Relaxing in a hammock on Wailea Beach.

Maui's **Farmlands**

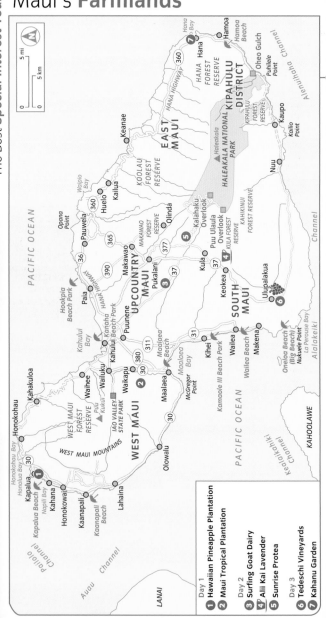

0   5 mi
0   5 km

Day 1
1 Hawaiian Pineapple Plantation
2 Maui Tropical Plantation

Day 2
3 Surfing Goat Dairy
4 Alii Kai Lavender
5 Sunrise Protea

Day 3
6 Tedeschi Vineyards
7 Kahanu Garden

When people think of Maui, flowers and leis often come to mind, but Maui's fertile soil grows lush fields of everything from tropical fruit and exotic flowers to breadfruit and lavender. The island even produces goat cheese and wine. Below are my favorite tours of Maui's bounty. START: **Kapalua. Trip length: 3 days and 116 miles (187km).**

1 Hawaiian Pineapple Plantation. Start with Hawaii's king of fruits by taking the 2-hour Hawaiian Pineapple Plantation Tour and learn about the pineapple's history and facts about its growing and harvesting cycles. ⏲ *2 hr. Kapalua Villas Reception Center, across from the Honolua Store, Office Rd., Kapalua.* ☎ *808/669-8088. www.kapaluamaui.com.*

Travel south on Hwy. 30 for 27 miles (43km). Allow about 40 to 45 minutes.

2 kids Maui Tropical Plantation. The Maui Tropical Plantation Tour is a 45- to 60-minute narrated tram tour of this 60-acre (24ha) working plantation that produces tropical fruits and flowers (papaya, guava, mango, macadamia nuts, coffee, avocado, bananas, sugar cane, star fruit, and more). Don't forget to stop by the store and pick up your favorite fruit. ⏲ *45–60 min. Btw. MM 2 and MM 3, on Hwy. 30, Waikapu.* ☎ *800/451-6805. www.mauitropicalplantation.com. Daily starting at 10am. Adults $14, children 3–12 $5.*

Head north on Hwy. 30, go right at the light on Main Street and continue through Wailuku and Kahului. Continue on Hwy. 36, take a right on Pulehu Road, and veer left on Omaopio Road, which is about a mile down on the right.

A luscious Maui pineapple.

Allow 30 to 40 minutes.

3 kids Surfing Goat Dairy. In Kula, just beyond the sugar-cane fields and on the slopes of Haleakala, lies this dairy, where some 140 dairy goats blissfully graze the 42 acres (17ha) and contribute the milk for the 24 different cheeses that are made every day. Choose from the 2-hour **Grand Dairy Tour ($25),** where you can learn how to milk a goat, make cheese, and sample the different varieties; or drop by for the 20-minute casual dairy tour ($7). ⏲ *20–120 min. 3651 Omaopio Rd., Kula.* ☎ *808/878-2870. Open Mon–Sat 10am–3:15pm, Sun 10am–1pm. www.surfinggoatdairy.com.*

Continue up Omaopio Road to Hwy. 37 and turn right. At your second left after Rice park, turn on Hwy. 377, drive about ¼ mile (.4km), rounding a bend and taking a quick right up Waipoli Road. Allow 20 to 30 minutes.

Head for lunch at **4 Ali'I Kula Lavender Maui,** where a variety of terrific tours take you to see the various varieties of lavender that bloom year-round. My favorite is the daily 50-minute Walking Tour, which explores the grounds. You can add a Lavender Gourmet Lunch Basket and taste the wonderful fruits of this farm as you gaze out

Wow! Look at the Size of That Fish

Enormous fish swim around the island of Maui. The largest, a Pacific blue marlin caught in Maui waters, tipped the scale at 1,200 pounds and was 15-feet (5m) long. If you want to see what Hawaii's big-game fish look like, wander down to the docks at Lahaina

or Maalaea either just after noon or around 5pm when the sportfishing boats return with their catch. At the end of October, the island's largest fishing tournament takes place in Lahaina, the **Lahaina Jackpot Fishing Tournament.** Some 75 teams compete to haul in the "big one." During the event, nightly fish weigh-ins take place at the Lahaina Harbor starting at 4pm. For more information contact the **Lahaina Yacht Club** (835 Front St., Lahaina; ☎ 808/661-0191; www.lahaina yachtclub.org).

People checking out the day's catch.

over the breathtaking view. *1100 Waipoli Rd., Kula.* ☎ *808/878-3004. www.aliikulalavender.com.*

Go right on Hwy. 377 to Hwy. 378. Allow about 15 minutes.

⑤ Sunrise Protea. After lunch, you'll have plenty of time to see Maui's most unusual flower, the other-worldly protea, which is actually native to South Africa. On Haleakala's rich volcanic slopes, Sunrise Protea offers a walk-through garden tour, a gift shop, friendly service, and a

Protea.

larger-than-usual selection of these exotic flowers. If you can swing it, go on a Tuesday or a Friday, when the just-cut flowers come in from the fields. 🕐 *1–2 hr. Haleakala Hwy., Kula.* ☎ *800/222-2797. www.sunriseprotea.com. Walking tour $12; walking tour and lunch basket $37.*

From Kula take Hwy. 378 to Hwy. 377, then make a left turn on Hwy. 37. The winery is another 12 miles (19km) down the road. Allow 30 to 45 minutes.

⑥ Tedeschi Vineyards. Plan to arrive in time for a free tour (10:30am,

Breadfruit.

1:30pm, or 3pm) of the grounds and wine-producing operation at Maui's only winery. Not only will you get to see the historic grounds, including the tasting room, which was the guest cottage built for King Kalakaua in 1874, but you'll also learn about the six different varietals grown on the slopes of Haleakala. ⏲ *1 hr. Ulu-palakua.* ☎ *877/878-6058. www. mauiwine.com. Tasting room open daily 9am–5pm.*

Take Hwy. 31 east to Hana. Just before MM 31, turn down Ulaino Road toward the ocean. Allow about 1 to 1½ hours driving time.

⑦ Kahanu Garden. The world's largest collection of breadfruit trees—a staple food crop for Pacific islanders—can be found here. The garden has some 130 distinct variet-ies gathered from 20 tropical island groups. Also here is the Canoe Gar-den, which assembles all the useful plants that the early Polynesian set-tlers brought to Hawaii: sugar cane, banana, sweet potato, taro, tur-meric, and paper mulberry (used to make *kapa* cloth). ⏲ *1–2 hr. Ulaino Rd. (turn toward the ocean at MM 31 off the Hana Hwy.).* ☎ *808/248-8912. www.ntbg.org/gardens/kahanu. Self-guided tours $10; guided tours: $25; children 12 and under free.*

Maui's Farmers' Market

If you want the freshest Maui fruits, flowers, and produce (at budget prices), show up at the farmers' market closest to where you're staying.

Kahului has two farmers' markets to choose from: One is held every Friday, from 8:30am to 2:30pm at the **Queen Ka'ahumanu Center** and the other is on Wednesday from 6am to 1pm at the **Kahului Shopping Center.** Just up the street, the Wailuku Farm-ers' Market, in the Maui County parking lot, on Market Street, in Wailuku, takes place Monday to Friday, from 8am to 6pm. If you are staying in the **Kihei** area, on Monday, Wednesday, and Friday, from 1 to 5pm, there's a farmers' market at the **Suda Store.** If you are staying anywhere from Lahaina to Kapalua, try the **Honokowai Farmers' Market,** on lower Honoapiilani Road, across from the Honokowai Park (near Haku Hale Place). It is open every Monday, Wednesday, and Friday, 7 to 11am.

Maui's **History & Culture**

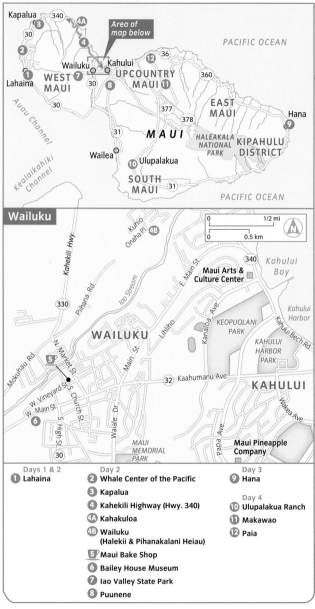

Wailuku

Days 1 & 2	Day 2	Day 3
1 Lahaina	**2** Whale Center of the Pacific	**9** Hana
	3 Kapalua	
	4 Kahekili Highway (Hwy. 340)	Day 4
	4A Kahakuloa	**10** Ulupalakua Ranch
	4B Wailuku (Halekii & Pihanakalani Heiau)	**11** Makawao
	5 Maui Bake Shop	**12** Paia
	6 Bailey House Museum	
	7 Iao Valley State Park	
	8 Puunene	

It is possible to walk back in time on Maui, back to the ancient Hawaiians who first came to the island, to the missionaries and whalers who arrived in the 1800s, to the plantation workers and cowboys of the 1900s, and most recently, to the hippies of the 1960s and 1970s. Plan to spend your first night in West Maui and your second night in Wailuku. START: **Lahaina. Trip length: 2 days and 75 miles (120.7km).**

1 Lahaina. This old town, whose name translates as "merciless sun," has archaeological evidence dating back to A.D. 700. If you've just arrived, a terrific way to dip your toes into Maui culture is at the **Old Lahaina Luau** (p 124). Head over to the **Baldwin Home Museum** to begin the Lahaina tour (p 50), which covers the days of the whalers and missionaries and their effect on Lahaina.

Take Hwy. 30 north to Kaanapali, a 5-minute drive.

2 Whale Center of the Pacific. For more on the whalers, stop by Whalers Village in Kaanapali, at this museum celebrating the "Golden Era of Whaling" (1825–1860). Harpoons and scrimshaw are on display and the museum has

even re-created the cramped quarters of a whaler's seagoing vessel. ⏱ *30 min. Whalers Village, 2435 Kaanapali Pkwy., Kaanapali.* ☎ *808/661-5992. www.whalersvillage.com. Free admission. Daily 9:30am–10pm.*

Continue north on Hwy. 30 to Kapalua, a 10- to 15-minute drive.

3 Kapalua. To go back even farther in time, drive out to Kapalua (two borders) where on the hill, on the ocean side of the Ritz-Carlton Kapalua, the burial sites of hundreds of ancient Hawaiians were discovered in the sand. The hotel, which was under construction at the time of the discovery, was moved inland to avoid disturbing the graves. You'll find a plaque here detailing their history.

Baldwin Home Museum.

Continue north, past Kapalua, on Hwy. 30 (which becomes Hwy. 340, then Hwy. 330, and then N. Market St.). Go left on Mills Street, left again on Lower Main Street, and follow this street until it ends at Hwy. 340, and make another left. Go left again on Kuhio Street and then take your first left on Hea Place, following it to the end. Allow 45 minutes to an hour to reach Wailuku.

❹ Kahekili Highway (Hwy. 340). Along this highway (named for the great chief Kahekili, who built houses from the skulls of his enemies), nestled in a crevice between two steep hills, is the picturesque village of **❹A Kahakuloa** (the tall hau tree), with a dozen weather-worn houses, a church with a red-tile roof, and vivid green taro patches. Life here has not changed much during the past few decades. Continue into **❹B Wailuku** to see two ancient sites: **Halekii** and **Pihanakalani Heiau**, built in 1240 from stones carried up from the Iao Stream below. Chief Kahekili lived

here. After the bloody battle at Iao Stream, Kamehameha I (the king who united the Hawaiian Islands) reportedly came to the temple here to pay homage to the war god, Ku, with a human sacrifice. Halekii (house of images) has stone walls and a flat grassy top, whereas Pihanakalani (gathering place of supernatural beings) is a pyramid-shaped mound of stones. If you sit quietly nearby (never walk on any *heiau*—it's considered disrespectful), you'll see that the view alone explains why this spot was chosen.

❺ Maui Bake Shop. Sure, you can buy a great smelling loaf of bread, baked in one of Maui's oldest brick ovens (dating to 1935), or one of the sumptuous fresh-fruit gâteaux, puff pastries, or dozens of other baked goods, but I recommend holding out for the white-chocolate macadamia-nut cheesecake. *2092 Vineyard St. (at N. Church St.), Wailuku.* ☎ *808/242-0064. $.*

Kahakuloa Village.

Eat Like a Local

Are you the type of visitor who feels you haven't "experienced" a destination unless you've hit the restaurants where the local residents eat? Or do you enjoy National Public Radio's *Road Food*, or any of the Food Network's on-the-road culinary shows? Then sign up for **Tour da Food** ★★★ (☎ 808/242-8383; www.tourdafood.com). Pastry chef (and food writer, restaurant publicist, and cookbook author) Bonnie Friedman takes foodies off the tourist path to discover the culinary treasures—from snack shacks and restaurants to markets and manufacturers—that make up Maui's unique cuisine. You will laugh your way across the island with Bonnie's wonderful commentary about Maui's multicultural food options and its colorful history—and you'll also eat some of the island's most yummy food (which you never would have discovered on your own). Check out her website to read about the different tours (from breakfast at an old inn to "lunch like a local" to "plate lunch and picnic with poke"); prices begin at $260 per couple, which includes transportation, a main meal, snacks, a traditional island dessert, a bag of goodies to take home, and Bonnie's personal list of under-the-radar eating places. *Tip:* Book this tour early in your trip, so you have time to follow Bonnie's terrific suggestions of places to eat on Maui. (Best to book at least 1 week in advance.)

Retrace your steps and turn left at North Market Street. Go right on Vineyard Street, and left on High Street. At the light, turn right on Main Street; Bailey House Museum is on the left.

⑥ ★★ Bailey House Museum. Moving forward both literally and historically, the next stop is the 1833 home of missionary and sugar planter Edward Bailey, containing one of my favorite treasure troves of Hawaiiana, with everything from scary temple images, dog-tooth necklaces, and a rare lei made of tree-snail shells, to latter-day relics like Duke Kahanamoku's 1919 redwood surfboard.

🕐 30–45 min. 2375-A Main St. ☎ 808/244-3326. www.maui museum.org. Admission $5 adults, $4 seniors, $1 children 7–12, free for children 6 and under. Mon–Sat 10am–4pm.

Continue up Main Street, which becomes Iao Valley Road, to the end.

⑦ Iao Valley State Park. It's hard to imagine that peaceful Iao Stream was the site of one of Maui's worst battles. In 1790 King Kamehameha the Great and his men fought at Iao Valley to gain control of Maui. When the battle ended, so many bodies

MAUI HISTORICAL SOCIETY

Bailey House MUSEUM

Mission Home
Hawaiian Artifacts
Museum Shop

Bailey House Museum sign.

A view of Upcountry Maui.

blocked the stream that the battle site was named Kepaniwai, or "damming of the waters." The park and stream get their names from the Iao Needle, a phallic rock that juts an impressive 2,250 feet (686m) above sea level. *Iao* in Hawaiian means "supreme light."

Iao Valley Needle.

Retrace your steps to Main Street and continue straight through Wailuku and Kahului. Turn right at the light on to South Puunene Avenue, and continue until Hansen Road in Puunene.

8 Puunene. In the middle of the central Maui plains, the town of Puunene (goose hill) has almost disappeared. Once a thriving sugar-plantation town with hundreds of homes, a school, a shopping area, and a community center, Puunene is now little more than a sugar mill, a post office, and the **Alexander & Baldwin Sugar Museum** (Puunene Ave./Hwy. 350 and Hansen Rd.; ☎ 808/871-8058; www.sugar museum.com). This former sugar-mill superintendent's home has been converted into a museum that tells the story of sugar in Hawaii, from how sugar is grown, harvested, and milled, to how Samuel Alexander and Henry Baldwin (founders of Maui's largest sugar plantation, HC&S) managed to acquire huge chunks of land from the Kingdom of Hawaii, then ruthlessly fought to gain access to water on the other side of the island, making sugar cane an economically viable crop. ●

4 The Best Regional & Town Tours

West Maui

0 Olowalu
2 Lahaina
3 Kaanapali
4 Kapalua

This is the fabled Maui you see on postcards: Jagged peaks, green valleys, crystal clear water, and sandy beaches. The stretch of coastline from Kapalua to the historic port of Lahaina is the island's busiest resort area (with South Maui a close second). Expect a few mainland-style traffic jams. START: **Olowalu. Trip length: 17 miles (27km).**

1 kids **Olowalu.** Most visitors drive right past this tiny hamlet, 5 miles (8km) south of Lahaina. If you blink, you'll miss the general store and **Chez Paul Restaurant** (p 123). Olowalu (many hills) was the scene of the 1790 massacre, when the Hawaiians stole a skiff from the USS *Eleanora,* and the captain of the ship retaliated by mowing them down with his cannons, killing 100 people and wounding many others. Stop at **MM 14,** for one of my

Previous page: Iao Valley.

favorite snorkeling spots—over a turtle-cleaning station about 150 to 225 feet (46–69m) out from shore— to see turtles lining up to have cleaner wrasses (small fish) pick parasites off their shells. Take at least 30 minutes to watch the turtles.

Take Hwy. 30 north 7 miles (11km).

2 ★★★ kids **Lahaina.** Plan a minimum of a half-day in Lahaina. See p 50.

Travel Tip

I've used the highway number, not the name of the highway, when detailing how to get around on Maui. The abbreviation MM stands for "mile marker." For more information, see "Maui Driving Tips" on p 13.

Take Hwy. 30 for 3 miles (4.8km) north of Lahaina.

3 Kaanapali. Hawaii's first master-planned resort consists of pricey midrise hotels, lining nearly 3 miles (4.8km) of gold-sand beach. Golf greens wrap around the slope between beachfront and hillside properties. Inside Kaanapali Resort, turn toward the ocean from Hwy. 30 on Kaanapali Parkway to reach **Whalers Village,** a seaside mall (for information on the stores here, see p 140), that has adopted the whale as its mascot. You can't miss the huge (almost life-size) metal sculpture of a mother whale and two nursing calves that greets you. The reason to stop here is the tiny museum inside Whalers Village, **Whale Center of the Pacific** (p 43), which celebrates the "Golden Era of Whaling" from 1825 to 1860. It's small, but packed with wonderful displays from harpoons to scrimshaw; my favorite exhibit is the re-created cramped quarters of a whaler's seagoing vessel (it will make you stop complaining about the size of your hotel room!). Self-guided audio tours and short videos are available throughout the day.

Continue north on Hwy. 30 for 7 miles (11km).

4 ★ Kapalua. As you continue on Hwy. 30, the vista opens up to fields of silver-green pineapple and manicured golf fairways. Turn down Office Road, a country lane bordered by Pacific pines marching toward the sea. This is the exclusive domain of the luxurious **Ritz-Carlton Kapalua** (p 116), located next to two bays that are marine-life preserves (with fabulous surfing in winter). The resort has a cultural center, a golf school, three golf courses (p 90), historic features, a collection of swanky condos and homes, and wide-open spaces that include a rainforest preserve—all open to the general public. Pack a picnic lunch and spend a day here.

Whale skeleton at Whalers Village.

Lahaina

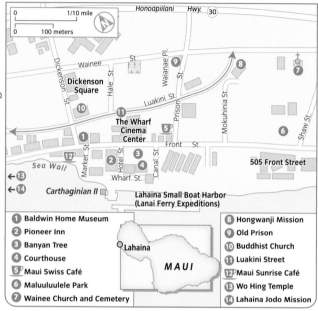

0 Baldwin Home Museum
2 Pioneer Inn
3 Banyan Tree
4 Courthouse
5 Maui Swiss Café
6 Maluuluulele Park
7 Wainee Church and Cemetery

8 Hongwanji Mission
9 Old Prison
10 Buddhist Church
11 Luakini Street
12 Maui Sunrise Café
13 Wo Hing Temple
14 Lahaina Jodo Mission

B etween the West Maui Mountains and the deep azure ocean offshore, Lahaina stands out as one of the few places in Hawaii that has managed to preserve its 19th-century heritage while still accommodating 21st-century guests. It has been the royal capital of Hawaii, the main center of the whaling industry, the place where missionaries tried to save the Hawaiians, the home of a sugar plantation, and today, one of the most popular towns in Maui for visitors to explore. START: **Baldwin Home Museum on Front Street. Trip length: 2 miles (3.2km).**

1 Baldwin Home Museum.
Start your journey back into the 19th century by stepping inside this coral and rock structure, the oldest house in Lahaina, and imagining what it must have been like to live here as a foreigner in 1834 when Rev. Dwight Baldwin, a doctor with the American missionaries, built it. Next-door is the **Masters' Reading Room,** Maui's oldest building. ⏱ 30 min. 120 Dickenson St. (at Front St.).

☎ 808/661-3262. www.lahaina restoration.org. Admission $3 adults, $2 seniors, $5 families, free for children ages 12 and under. Daily 10am–4:30pm.

2 Pioneer Inn. Wander into Lahaina's first hotel, which looks pretty much the way it did when it was built in 1901. If the walls of this old building could talk, they would be singing about some pretty wild parties at the turn of the 20th century. George Freeland, of the Royal Canadian Mounted Police, tracked a criminal to Lahaina and then fell in love with the town, building this hotel, which is still open for business. You can also get a cold drink at the old bar on the south side of the hotel and watch the goings-on at the harbor. ⏲ *30 min., if you stop for a drink. 658 Wharf St.* ☎ *808/661-3636. www.pioneerinnmaui.com.*

❸ **kids** **Banyan Tree.** This is every kid's dream—a tree made for climbing. Of all the banyan trees in Hawaii, this is the largest, so big that you can't get it in your camera's viewfinder. It was only 8 feet (2.4m) tall when it was planted in 1873 by Maui sheriff William O. Smith to mark the 50th anniversary of Lahaina's first Christian mission. Now it's more than 50 feet (15m) tall, has 12 major trunks, and shades 2/3 of an acre (.27ha) in Courthouse Square. You can sit down in the shade and people-watch for a few minutes. ⏲ *15 min., if you have kids. At the Courthouse Bldg., 649 Wharf St.*

❹ **Courthouse.** This building served not only as a courthouse, but also as a custom house, post office, tax collector's office, and government offices. Although it looks stuffy on the outside, be sure and go up to the second floor to visit the **Lahaina Heritage Museum,** which has exhibits on the history and culture of Lahaina. My favorite is the three-dimensional relief map of Maui, a bird's-eye view of the island's topography. ⏲ *20 min. 648 Wharf St., Lahaina.* ☎ *808/661-1959. www.visitlahaina.com. Free admission. Daily 9am–5pm.*

❺ **Maui Swiss Café.** This is a great place for tropical smoothies, strong espresso, and affordable snacks. You can sit in the somewhat funky garden area, or (my preference) get your drink to go and wander over to the seawall to watch the surfers. *640 Front St.* ☎ *808/661-6776. $.*

❻ **Maluuluolele Park.** Though not much to look at now, this park and ball field was once a sacred stop for Hawaiians. It used to be a village, Mokuhinia, with a revered pond that was the home of a *moo* (a spirit in the form of a lizard), which the royal family honored as their personal guardian spirit. I recommend this stop because it can help visitors

Pioneer Inn.

A gravestone in Wainee Cemetery.

appreciate how the Hawaiians feel about the destruction of their culture and religion. (Imagine the Statue of Liberty being torn down and replaced with a dusty ball park.) ⏱ *5–10 min. Front/Shaw sts.*

7 Wainee Church and Cemetery. The first stone church in Hawaii (1828–32) was built here. The current church has been standing since 1953. Be sure to walk around to the back of the church: The row of palm trees on the ocean side includes some of the oldest palm trees in Lahaina. Next-door is the first Christian cemetery in Hawaii, the Wainee Cemetery, established in 1823. It tells a fascinating story of old Hawaii, with graves of Hawaiian chiefs, commoners, missionaries, and their families (infant mortality was high then), and sailors. ⏱ *10–15 min. Wainee/Shaw sts.*

8 Hongwanji Mission. This temple was originally built in 1910 by members of Lahaina's Buddhist sect. The current building was constructed in 1927, housing a temple and a language school. Although the church is not always open, the reverend who lives next-door takes the time to talk to visitors and will give a tour of the church to those who are interested. ⏱ *5 min., longer if you get a tour inside. Wainee/Luakini sts.*

9 Old Prison. The Hawaiians called the prison Hale Paahao (stuck in irons house). Sailors who refused to return to their boats at sunset were sent here. If the doors are open, wander inside and see the brick-walled area surrounding the center courtyard. Unfortunately it seems to be closed most days. ⏱ *5 min. Wainee/Prison sts.*

10 Buddhist Church. Most likely it will be closed, but this green wooden Shingon Buddhist temple is typical of the myriad Buddhist churches that sprang up all over the island when Japanese laborers were brought to work in the sugarcane fields. ⏱ *2 min. Luakini/Hale sts.*

11 Luakini Street. Sometimes to experience Hawaii you have to feel with your heart, and not "look" with your eyes. This is one of those places. "Luakini" translates as a *heiau* (temple) where the ruling chiefs prayed and where human sacrifices were made. This street received its unforgettable name after serving as the route for the funeral procession of Princess Harriet Nahienaena, sister of kings Kamehameha II and III. The princess was a victim of the rapid changes in Hawaiian culture. A convert to Protestantism, she fell in love with her brother at an early age. Just 20 years earlier, their relationship would have been nurtured in order to preserve the purity of the royal bloodlines. The missionaries, however, frowned on a brother and sister marrying. In August 1836 the couple had a son, who lived only a few short hours. Nahienaena never recovered and died in December of that same year. The route of her funeral procession through the breadfruit and koa trees to the cemetery became known as Luakini, in reference to the gods "sacrificing" the beloved princess. Stop on this street in the shade of one of the big breadfruit trees, and try to imagine the sorrow and fear of a population in transition. The old ways were dying—and the new ways were foreign and frightening.

Wo Hing Temple.

12 **Maui Sunrise Café.** Take a break at this tiny cafe on Front Street, next door to the library. Grab a cup of java and one of their delicious baked goods and relax in the patio garden out back. *693A Front St., Lahaina.* ☎ *808/661-8558. $.*

13 **Wo Hing Temple.** I love this temple; it's so well preserved that you'd swear they're just getting ready to hold a Saturday social. The Chinese were among the various immigrants brought to Hawaii to work in the sugar-cane fields. In 1909 several Chinese workers formed the Wo Hing society, a chapter of the Chee Kun Tong society, which dates from the 17th century. In 1912 they built this social hall for the Chinese community.

Great Buddha statue.

Completely restored, the Wo Hing Temple contains displays and artifacts on the history of the Chinese in Lahaina. Be sure to wander next-door to the cookhouse and watch the old movies of Hawaii taken by Thomas Edison in 1898 and 1903. 🕐 *20 min. Front St. (btw. Wahie Lane and Papalaua St.).* ☎ *808/661-3262. Admission $2 adults, free for children ages 12 and under. Daily 10am–4pm.*

14 **Lahaina Jodo Mission.** The first thing you'll see when you enter the grounds is the Great Buddha statue (some 12-ft./3.7m high and weighing 3½ tons). Seeing the Buddha is worth the trip alone. This site was sacred to the Hawaiians who called it Puunoa Point, meaning "the hill freed from taboo." Once a small village named Mala (garden), this peaceful place became a haven for Japanese immigrants. In 1968, on the 100th anniversary of the Japanese arrival in Hawaii, the giant Buddha statue was brought here from Japan. 🕐 *10–15 min. 12 Ala Moana St. (off Front St., near the Mala Wharf).* ☎ *808/661-4304. Free admission. Daily during daylight hours.*

South Maui

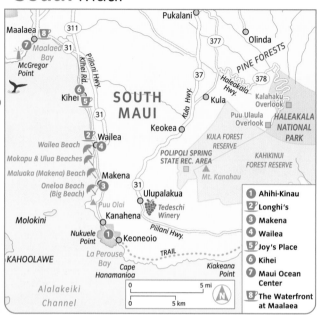

1. Ahihi-Kinau
2. Longhi's
3. Makena
4. Wailea
5. Joy's Place
6. Kihei
7. Maui Ocean Center
8. The Waterfront at Maalaea

To really see the hottest, sunniest, driest coastline on Maui—Arizona by the sea—you have to get out of your car and walk, paddle along the ocean in a kayak, or get in the water. You cannot experience this oceanside area merely by looking out the window as you drive by. On former scrubland from Maalaea to Makena, where cacti once grew wild and cows grazed, are now four distinct areas—Maalaea, Kihei, Wailea, and Makena—and a surprising amount of traffic. START: `Ahini-Kina`u Natural Area Reserve. Trip length: 20 miles (32km), but allow a full day to truly experience Maui's southern shore.

Travel Tip

Before you start this tour, pack a swimsuit, towels, good hiking shoes, sunscreen, a hat, plenty of water and (depending on what you want to do) maybe rent snorkel gear and/or a kayak (see chapter 6 for rental recommendations). Be sure to get up early to avoid the hot sun; you'll want to start off before 7am in the winter and 6am in the summer for the most comfortable temperatures.

Drive south on Makena Road, past Puu Olai to Ahihi Bay, where the road turns to gravel. Go another 2 miles (3.2km) along the coast to La Pérouse Bay.

1 ★ `Ahihi-Kina`u Natural Area Reserve. La Pérouse Monument is a pyramid of lava rocks that marks the spot where the first Westerner to "discover" the island, French explorer admiral comte de La Pérouse, set foot on Maui in 1786. Park here, and if you're up for it, start your hike. Bring plenty of water and sun protection, and wear hiking boots that can withstand walking on lava. From La Pérouse Bay, you can pick up the old **King's Highway trail,** which once circled the island. Walk along the sandy beach at La Pérouse; if the water is calm, take a swim, but if it's rough, just enjoy the view. Look for the trail indentation in the lava at the end of the sandy beach, which leads down to the lighthouse at the tip of Cape Hanamanioa, about .75 mile (1.2km) round-trip. Give yourself an hour or two to spend in the peace and quiet of this wilderness area. For current information on which sections are open to the public see the box below.

`Ahihi-Kina`u

As we went to press, the Hawaii State Department of Land and Natural Resources had temporarily restricted access to portions of the `Ahihi-Kina`u Natural Area Reserve until July 31, 2010. For a downloadable brochure on what's open and what's not, e-mail ahihikinauinfo@ hawaii.gov, or call ☎ 808/984-8100 for current information on the restrictions.

Retrace your route back to Makena Road. Veer right onto Makena Alanui Road, which becomes Wailea Alnui Road at the Shops at Wailea, about 3 miles (4.8km).

2 Longhi's. I love to sit in the open air and sip a latte and munch on Longhi's fresh-baked cinnamon rolls (one is enough for 2 people). Big eaters may want to try the eggs Benedict or Florentine with a light but flavorful hollandaise and perfect baguettes. *Shops at Wailea, 3750 Wailea Alanui Dr., Wailea.* ☎ *808/ 891-8883. $$.*

Retrace your route back to Makena Road and head toward Makena Landing Beach Park, a distance of 2 miles (3.2km).

3 ★ Makena. This beach park with boat-launching facilities, showers, toilets, and picnic tables, has generally calm waters teeming with colorful tropical fish. It's the perfect place for beginner kayakers and snorkelers. Dino Ventura of **Makena Kayak Tours** (p 104), specializes in teaching first-time kayakers. For one of the more history-rich

A sunrise view from `Ahihi-Kina`u Natural Area Reserve.

Maui's Early History

The first Hawaiian settlers arrived by canoe, part of the great Polynesian migration. No one is sure when they arrived, but artifacts at the Maluuluolele Park in Lahaina date back to between A.D. 700 and 900.

All we have today are archaeological finds, some scientific data, and ancient chants to tell the story of Hawaii's past. The chants, especially the *Kumulipo*, which is the chant of creation and the litany of genealogy of the *alii* (high-ranking chiefs) who ruled the islands, talk about journeys between Hawaii and the islands of the south, presumed to be Tahiti.

Around 1300, the transoceanic voyages stopped and Hawaii began to develop its own culture. The settlers built temples, fishponds, and aqueducts to irrigate taro plantations. Each island was a separate kingdom. The *alii* created a caste system and established taboos. High priests asked the gods Lono and Ku for divine guidance. Ritual human sacrifices were common.

Maui's history is one of wars and conquests, with one chief capturing another's land. The rugged terrain of Maui and the water separating Maui, Molokai, Lanai, and Kahoolawe made good natural boundaries. In the early years there were three kingdoms on Maui: Hana, Waikulu, and Lahaina.

In the early 15th century, a ruler from Hana became the first to unite Maui. Piilani's rule was a time of peace; he built fishponds and irrigation fields and began creating a paved road around the island.

stops in this area, go south on Makena Road from the landing; on the right is **Keawali Congregational Church ★** (☎ 808/879-5557), built in 1855. Surrounded by ti leaves, which by Hawaiian custom provide protection, and built of 3-foot (.9m) thick lava rock with coral for mortar, this Protestant church sits in its own cove with a golden-sand beach. It's not always open, but you can view the inside on Sunday during the 9:30am Hawaiian-language service. Take some time to wander through the cemetery, where you'll see some tombstones with ceramic pictures of the deceased, an old custom.

Retrace your route back to Makena Road. Go left on Makena Alanui Road, which becomes Wailea Alnui Road. Look for the blue sign noting PUBLIC BEACH ACCESS. It's in about 2 miles (3.2km).

4 ★ Wailea. Leaving the past in Makena, we're on to the present with the multimillion-dollar high-rise luxury resorts that line the 2 miles (3.2km) of this palm-fringed gold coast. For an up-close look, park in the public beach access lot and walk the oceanfront, 3-mile (4.8km) round-trip path, which has terrific views of both the ocean and the lushly landscaped resorts. Allow about an hour for this stroll along Maui's most expensive properties.

Go left on Wailea Alanui Road and left again at stop sign to Okolani Drive, which becomes Kihei Road. It's about 3½ miles (5.6km).

5 kids Joy's Place. Stop for lunch at this tiny eatery with healthy, delicious lunches (huge sandwiches, wraps, fresh salads, soups, and desserts) at rock-bottom prices. My picks are the falafel burger or the spinach quinoa burger. The deli has a few seats, but the beach is just across the street. *Island Surf Bldg., 1993 S. Kihei Rd., Kihei (entrance to the restaurant is on Auhana St.).* ☎ *808/879-9258.$.*

Continue north on Kihei Road for 2½ miles (4km).

6 Kihei. Kihei is a nearly continuous series of condos and minimalls lining Kihei Road. However, a couple of terrific places showcase island wildlife. To get some background on the whales that visit Hawaii from December to April, stop by the

Hawaii Humpback Whale Sanctuary Center (725 Kihei Rd.; ☎ 808/879-2818; www.hawaiihumpbackwhale.noaa.gov). This small educational center has dozens of exhibits, artifacts, and displays on whales, turtles, and other ocean life. Allow about 30 minutes here, then continue on Kihei Road north to **Kealia Pond National Wildlife Preserve** (☎ 808/875-1582), a 700-acre (283ha) U.S. Fish and Wildlife wetland preserve. This is a fantastic place to see many endangered Hawaiian species, like the black-crowned high heron and Hawaiian stilts, coots, and ducks. The best time to visit is from July to December, when hawksbill turtles come ashore to lay their eggs. You can take a self-guided tour along a boardwalk dotted with interpretive signs and shade shelters, through sand dunes, and around ponds to Maalaea Harbor. The boardwalk starts at the outlet of Kealia Pond on the ocean side of North Kihei Road (near MM 2 on Hwy. 31). Allow at

Wildlife at Kealia Pond.

Maui Ocean Center.

least an hour, longer if the turtles are around.

Continue north on Hwy. 31, then go left on Hwy. 30 to the Maalaea turn off. It's about 3 miles (4.8km).

7 ★★★ kids **Maui Ocean Center.** The windy oceanfront village of Maalaea centers on a small boat harbor (with a general store, a couple of restaurants, and a huge new mall) and the Maui Ocean Center, an aquarium/ocean complex. This 5-acre (2ha) facility houses the largest aquarium in Hawaii. My favorite section is the aquarium's centerpiece: a 100-foot-long (30m), 750,000-gallon tank featuring tiger, gray, and white-tip sharks, as well as tuna, surgeonfish, triggerfish, and numerous tropical fish. The aquarium is set up so you feel as though you are descending from the beach to the deepest part of the ocean. A walkway goes right through the tank, so you're surrounded on three sides by marine creatures. If you're a certified scuba diver, you can participate in the **Shark Dive Maui**

Program, which allows you (for a fee of $190) to plunge into the aquarium and swim with the sharks, stingrays, and tropical fish. ⏱ *2 hr. or more. Maalaea Harbor Village, 192 Maalaea Rd. (the triangle btw. Honoapiilani Hwy. and Maalaea Rd.).* ☎ *808/270-7000. www.maui oceancenter.com. Buy your tickets online to avoid long lines. Admission $25 adults, $22 seniors, $18 children 3–12. Daily 9am–5pm (until 6pm July–Aug).*

8 kids **The Waterfront at Maalaea.** Stop for dinner at this family-owned restaurant, known for its fresh seafood, which is caught in nearby Maalaea Harbor. I recommend any of the fresh fish (with nine different preparations). Vegetarian and meat entrees are also available. Dessert is baked fresh daily; my favorite is the double-chocolate brownie with vanilla ice cream. Try to come around sunset, when the harbor views are stunning. *Reservations are recommended. Maalaea Harbor, 50 Hauoli St.* ☎ *808/244-9028. $$$.*

How to Fit in Like a Local

Most visitors to Hawaii want to fit in and not be an "ugly American" tourist. The best way to do that is to be friendly and practice the same common courtesy that you do in your own neighborhood. If you smile and are polite to local residents, chances are they will smile back at you. Here are a few things you might want to consider:

- Be super polite when driving. People in Hawaii do not use their car horn as a comment on other people's driving. Most Hawaii residents use their car horn only as a greeting to a friend.
- Another driving comment—you may be on vacation, but not everyone living here is on vacation, so check your rearview mirror. If you are impeding traffic by driving slowly, pull off the road. If you want to watch the sunset, pull off the road. If you have a long line of cars behind you, pull off the road.
- Be respectful. Just because Maui is warm, this does not mean that it is acceptable to wear your swimwear into a restaurant. A good rule of thumb is to ask yourself: Would I wear this outfit at home to my neighborhood restaurant or retail store?
- Remember Hawaii is part of the United States and is in fact a state. A good way to alienate local residents is to say "I'm from the States" or "back in the States, we do it this way."

Maluaka (Makena) Beach.

Central Maui

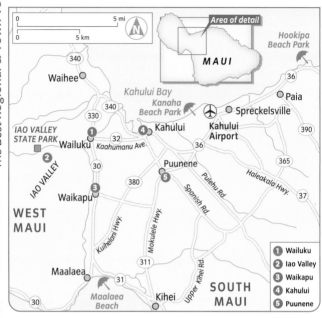

This flat, often windy corridor between Maui's two volcanoes is the site of the main airport, where you'll probably arrive. It's also home to the majority of the island's population, the heart of the business community, and center of the local government (courts, cops, and county/state government agencies). You'll find good shopping and dining bargains as well. START: **Wailuku. Trip length: 2½ miles (4km).**

1 ★ **Wailuku.** With its faded wooden storefronts, old plantation homes, and shops straight out of the 1940s, quaint little Wailuku is worth a brief visit for its history and architecture. Take a couple of hours to wander around. See p 44.

Take Main Street west to Valley Road, about 3½ miles (5.6km).

2 ★★ kids **Iao Valley.** A 2,250-foot (686m) needle pricks the sky. The air is moist and cool, and the shade a welcome comfort. This is Iao Valley (*Iao*

means "supreme light"), the eroded volcanic caldera of the West Maui Mountains and a 6-acre (2.4ha) state park. The head of the Iao Valley is a broad circular amphitheater where four major streams converge into **Iao Stream** (a great place for kids to splash around). At the back of the amphitheater is rain-drenched **Puu Kukui**, the West Maui Mountains' highest point. No other Hawaiian valley lets you go from seacoast to rainforest so easily. This peaceful valley, full of tropical plants, rainbows, waterfalls, swimming holes, and hiking trails (two of them paved and easy), is a place of solitude, reflection, and escape. Pack a picnic, take your swimsuit, and spend a couple of hours. *Iao Valley State Park, 54 S. High St., Wailuku.* ☎ *808/984-8109. Open daily 10am–4pm.*

Retrace your route to the light at Main Street and Hwy. 30, turn right and drive 3 miles (4.8km) south on Hwy. 30.

③ **Kids Waikapu.** The tiny, single-street village of Waikapu has at least one attraction that's worth checking out: the 40-minute narrated tram ride around fields of pineapple, sugar cane, and papaya trees at Maui Tropical Plantation (p 39) that allows you to relive Maui's past. Make sure that you have at least an hour to spend here; you'll want to check out the country store before you leave.

Head north on Hwy. 30, go right on Waiko Road (Hwy. 305), and go left on Hwy. 380 to Kahului. Parking for the Kanana Wildlife Sanctuary is behind the mall, across from Cutter Automotive, where Hwy. 37 and Hwy. 36 intersect. It's about 4 miles (6.4km).

④ **Kahului.** As you drive through Maui's most populated town, look out on the miles of subdivisions: This is "Dream City," home to thousands of former sugar-cane workers who dreamed of owning their own homes away from the plantations. Despite a few shopping opportunities (p 133), this is not a place to spend your vacation. However, one attraction that is worth visiting—incongruously located under the airport flight path, next to Maui's busiest intersection and across from Costco in Kahului's new business park—is the **Kanaha Wildlife Sanctuary** (Haleakala Hwy. Ext. and Hana Hwy.; ☎ 808/984-8100). A 150-foot (46m) trail meanders along the shore to a shade shelter and lookout to the permanent home of the endangered

black-neck Hawaiian stilt, whose population is now down to about 1,000 to 1,500. Naturalists say this is a good place to see endangered Hawaiian ducks, stilts, coots, and other migrating shorebirds. Plan a quick 10-minute drive through the town and another 15 minutes wandering the wildlife sanctuary.

Take Hwy. 36 to the intersection, go right on Daily Road, left on Puunene Avenue, and left on Hansen Road. It's about 2 miles (3.2km).

⑤ **Puunene.** To soak up a little more of Maui's colorful history, drive out to this town in the middle of the central Maui plains. Once a thriving sugar-plantation town with hundreds of homes, a school, a shopping area, and a community center, Puunene today consists of little more than a sugar mill, a post office, and a museum (the **Alexander & Baldwin Sugar Museum,** p 46). You can tour the museum in 15 minutes, then step outside, breathe in the smells of the nearby sugar mill, and watch the green sugar cane blowing in the wind. This is a part of Maui that is quickly disappearing.

Iao Valley.

Upcountry Maui

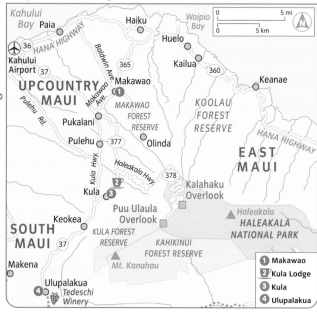

After a few days at the beach, you'll probably be ready to explore the 10,000-foot (3,048km) mountain in the middle of Maui. The slopes of Haleakala are home to cowboys, farmers, and other welcoming country people. Crisp air, emerald pastures, eucalyptus, flower farms, even a misty California redwood grove are the highlights of this tropical Olympus. START: **Makawao. Trip length: 24 miles (42km), but plan on a full day.**

1 ★ **Makawao.** Until recently, this small, two-street town consisted of little more than a post office, a gas station, a feed store, a bakery, a restaurant/bar, and hitching posts for horses. As the population of Maui started expanding in the 1970s, however, a health-food store popped up, followed by boutiques and a host of health-conscious restaurants. The result is an eclectic amalgam of old *paniolo* (cowboy) Hawaii and the baby-boomer trends of transplanted mainlanders. Spend the morning

looking at the unusual shops. Don't miss my favorite, **Hui No'eau Visual Arts Center** (p 136), Hawaii's premier arts collective.

Take Makawao Avenue to the light at Hwy. 37, turn left, and head up the mountain. Go left on Hwy. 377. It will take about 25 minutes.

2 **Kula Lodge.** Take a lunch break here not only for the food, but also for the million-dollar vista that spans the flanks of Haleakala, central Maui, the ocean, and the West Maui Mountains. My favorites are the Kula onion soup (with Maui's famous sweet onions) and the clubhouse sandwich (smoked turkey on a homemade bun with homemade spicy orange barbecue sauce). *Haleakala Hwy. (Hwy. 377).* ☎ *808/878-2517. $$.*

Retrace your route on Hwy. 377, then go left on Hwy. 37. It's a 5-minute drive to Ali'i Kula Lavender, and about 20 to 30 minutes from there to Surfing Goat Dairy.

❸ ★ **Kula.** Continue south through the bucolic rolling hills of this pastoral upcountry community of old flower farms, humble cottages, and new suburban ranch houses with million-dollar views that take in the ocean, isthmus, West Maui Mountains, Lanai, and Kahoolawe off in the distance. Kula sits at a cool 3,000 feet (914m), just below the cloud line, and from here a winding road snakes its way up to Haleakala National Park. Everyone in this area grows something—Maui onions, carnations, orchids, and proteas, those strange-looking blossoms that look like *Star Trek* props. Must stops

are: **Ali'i Kula Lavender** (p 32) and **Surfing Goat Dairy** (p 39).

Continue on Hwy. 37 for 14 miles (23km).

❹ ★ **Ulupalakua.** The final stop on the upcountry tour is on the southern shoulder of Haleakala, **Ulupalakua Ranch,** a 20,000-acre (8,094ha) spread once owned by legendary sea captain James Makee. The ranch is now home to Maui's only **winery,** established in 1974 by Napa vintner Emil Tedeschi. Stop in the tasting room and sample Maui's wines (pass on the pineapple wines—Maui Splash and Maui Blanc—yuck!). Across from the winery are the remains of the three smokestacks of the **Makee Sugar Mill,** built in 1878. This is home to Maui artist Reems Mitchell, who carved the mannequins on the front porch of the Ulupalakua Ranch Store: a Filipino with his fighting cock, a cowboy, a farmhand, and a sea captain, all representing the people of Maui's history. (When you drive past you'll swear they're real.) *Tedeschi Vineyards and Winery, off Hwy. 37 (Kula Hwy.).* ☎ *808/878-6058. www.mauiwine.com. Daily 9am–5pm. Free tastings; free tours given 10:30am–1:30pm.*

Hui No'eau Visual Arts Center.

The **Road to Hana**

1 Kahului
2 Charley's
3 Hookipa Beach Park
4 Jaws
5 Maui Grown Market and Deli
6 Twin Falls
7 Huelo
8 Waikamoi Ridge
9 Kaumahina State Wayside Park
10 Keanae Arboretum
11 Keanae Peninsula
12 Keanae Lookout
13 Uncle Harry's Fruit & Flower Stand
14 Wailua
15 Wailua Valley State Wayside Park
16 Puaa Kaa State Wayside Park
17 Nahiku
18 Nahiku Coffee Shop

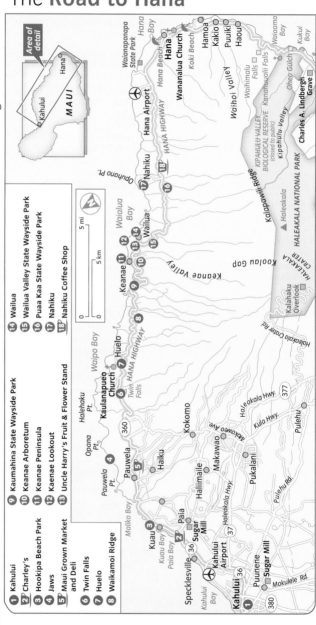

Top down, sunscreen on, swimsuit handy, radio tuned to a Hawaiian music station on a Maui morning: It's time to head out to Hana along the Hana Highway (Hwy. 36). This wiggle of a road winds for 50 miles (80km) along Maui's northeastern shore, passing taro patches, magnificent seascapes, waterfall pools, botanical gardens, and verdant rainforests. Bring a few beach towels, a picnic lunch, and your camera. START: **Kahului. Trip length: 50 miles (80km). The drive takes at least 3 hours, but to really enjoy the trip, plan to spend all day.**

1 Fueling up in Kahului. This is the cheapest place to get gas. Don't wait until Paia, the last place for gas before the long trip to Hana, because it's incredibly expensive.

Continue on the Hana Highway for 8 miles (13km).

2 kids Charley's. Pull into quaint Paia for a big, hearty breakfast at Charley's for a reasonable price. *142 Hana Hwy., Paia.* ☎ *808/579-9453. $–$$.*

Continue on the Hana Highway until just before MM 9.

3 ★ kids Hookipa Beach Park. *See p 76.*

Detour off the Hana Highway left at Hahana Road, between MM 13 and 14. Don't park on the pineapples!

4 ★★ kids Jaws. If it's winter and conditions are right, expert tow-in surfers battle the mammoth waves off Pauwela at an area known as Jaws (because the waves will chew you up).

Just before MM 15:

5 Maui Grown Market and Deli. This is my pick for the best bang-for-your-buck picnic lunch: A mere $8.95 gets you a sandwich (my favorite is the avo-veggie, but they also have pastrami, roast beef,

The Road to Hana.

turkey, and tuna), with two cookies, a mac-nut candy bar, chips or fruit, and soda or water. *Hana Hwy.* ☎ *808/572-1693. $.*

After MM 16, the road is still called the Hana Highway, but the number changes from Hwy. 36 to Hwy. 360, and the mile markers go back to 0. Stop at MM 2.

6 Twin Falls. Pull over on the mountainside and park; the waterfall and pool are a 3- to 5-minute walk. The mountain stream water is a bit chilly when you first get in, but it's good for swimming. If it's crowded, keep going, plenty of other swimming holes and waterfalls are coming up.

Make sure to pull off at a waterfall or two for an impromptu swim.

Just before MM 4, on a blind curve, look for a double row of mailboxes on the left.

7 Huelo. This is a great side trip to see some of Maui's history. Down the road lies a hidden Hawaii, where an indescribable sense of serenity prevails. Hemmed in by Waipo and Hoalua bays is the remote community of Huelo. This fertile area once supported a population of 75,000; today only a few hundred live here. Stop in at the historic 1853 **Kaulanapueo Church.**

Continue to MM 9.

8 kids Waikamoi Ridge. This small state wayside area with restrooms, picnic tables, and a barbecue area has an easy .75-mile (1.2km) loop-trail hike. It starts just behind the QUIET TREES AT WORK sign.

An overview of the Keanae Peninsula.

Just past MM 12:

9 kids Kaumahina State Wayside Park. This is not only a good pit stop (restrooms are available) and a wonderful place for the picnic you picked up earlier, but it also offers wonderful views and a great photo op of the rugged coastline all the way down to the jutting Keanae Peninsula.

Between MM 16 and MM 17:

10 ★★ kids Keanae Arboretum. Here the region's botany is divided into three parts: native forest; introduced forest; and traditional Hawaiian plants, food, and medicine. You can swim in the pools of Piinaau Stream or walk a mile-long (1.6km) trail into Keanae Valley's tropical rainforest.

11 ★★★ kids Keanae Peninsula. The old Hawaiian village of **Keanae** stands out against the Pacific like a place time forgot. This is one of the last coastal enclaves of native Hawaiians. Be sure to visit the **Keanae Congregational Church** (☎ 808/248-8040). Built in 1860 of lava rocks and coral mortar, it stands in stark contrast to the surrounding green fields.

Just past MM 17:

12 kids Keanae Lookout. Get the camera out: Here you can see the entire Keanae Peninsula's checkerboard pattern of green taro fields and its ocean boundary etched in black lava.

Around MM 18:

13 Uncle Harry's Fruit & Flower Stand. Around MM 18 you'll start to see numerous small stands selling fruit or flowers. Many stands work on the honor system. My favorite, Uncle Harry's, sells a variety of fruits and juices Monday through Saturday.

Just after Uncle Harry's, look for the Wailua Road off on the left.

14 **Wailua.** Behind pink St. Gabriel's Church is the smaller, blue-and-white **Coral Miracle Church,** home of the **Our Lady of Fatima Shrine.** According to legend, in 1860 the men of this village were diving to collect coral to build a church. But the coral offshore was in deep water and the men could only retrieve a few pieces at a time, making construction an arduous project. Then a freak storm hit the area and deposited the deep-sea coral on a nearby beach, allowing the Hawaiians to easily complete the church.

Just before MM 19:

15 ★ kids **Wailua Valley State Wayside Park.** Climb the stairs for a view of the Keanae Valley, waterfalls, and Wailua Peninsula. On a really clear day, you can see up the mountain to the Koolau Gap.

Between MM 22 and MM 23:

16 kids **Puaa Kaa State Wayside Park.** The sound of waterfalls provides the background music for this small park area with restrooms, a phone, and a picnic area. There's a well-marked path to the falls and to a swimming hole. Ginger plants are everywhere: Pick some flowers along the highway and put them in your car so that you can travel with their sweet smell.

Just after MM 25 is a narrow 3-mile (4.8km) road leading from the highway, at about 1,000 feet (305m) elevation, down to sea level.

17 **Nahiku.** This remote, stunningly beautiful area was once a thriving village of thousands; today the population has dwindled to fewer than a hundred—including a few Hawaiian families, but mostly extremely wealthy mainland residents who jet in for a few weeks at a time. At the end of the road, you can see the remains of the old wharf from the town's rubber-plantation days. There's a small picnic area off to the side. Dolphins are frequently seen in the bay.

Go ½ mile (.8km) past MM 28 on the ocean side of the road.

18 **Nahiku Coffee Shop.** What a delight to stumble across this small coffee shop with locally made baked goods, Maui-grown coffee, banana bread, organic tropical-fruit smoothies, and my favorite, the Original and Best Coconut Candy. While you are here, check out the Smoked Fish Stand, a great place to stock up on superb smoked and grilled fish. Next-door the Ti Gallery sells locally made Hawaiian arts and crafts. *Hana Hwy., ½ mile past MM 28. No phone. $.*

A fruit stand on the way to Hana.

Hana

To Hana Airport & Kahului

Hana-Waianapanapa Trail

Kainalimu Bay

Nanualele Point

(See map below)

Hana Hwy.

Kawaipapa Stream

360

Wakoloa Rd.

Hana Medical Center

Police Station

360

Hana Hwy.

Ua Kea Rd.

Hana Bay

Kauki St.

Alau

5

Puukii Island

Puu O Kahaula (Lyon's Hill) (545 ft.)

Keanini Dr.

3

Hana Beach Park

Keawa Pl.

6

Hana Ballpark

Hana Community Center

Kauiki Head

7

Hauoli Rd.

8

Red Sand Beach

Mill Pl.

9

4

Kaihalulu Bay

360

Hana Hwy.

1 Kahanu Garden
2 Waianapanapa State Park
3 Hana Cultural Center and Museum
4 Hasegawa General Store
5 Hana Bay
6 Hotel Hana-Maui
7 Fagan's Cross
8 Wananalua Congregation Church
9 Hana Ranch Center
10 Oheo Gulch
11 Lindbergh's Grave
12 Kaupo

| 0 | 1/4 mi |
| 0 | 0.25 km |

N

(See map below)

10 11 12

Kapalua

PACIFIC OCEAN

30

340

Lahaina

WEST MAUI

Wailuku

36

30

Kahului

360

30

UPCOUNTRY MAUI

Area of map above

Auau Channel

377

EAST MAUI

1

378

2

Hana

MAUI

31

HALEAKALA NATIONAL PARK

KIPAHULU DISTRICT

Wailea

SOUTH MAUI

12

10

Kealaikahiki Channel

31

11

PACIFIC OCEAN

Green, tropical Hana is a destination all its own, a small coastal village that's probably what you came to Maui in search of. Here you'll find a rainforest punctuated with cascading waterfalls and sparkling blue pools, skirted by red- and black-sand beaches. Hana enjoys more than 90 inches of rain a year—more than enough to keep the scenery lush. Banyans, bamboo, breadfruit trees—everything seems larger than life in this small town, especially the wild ginger and plumeria flowers. Most visitors will zip through Hana, perhaps taking a quick look out their car windows at a few sights before buzzing on down the road. They might think they've seen Hana, but they definitely haven't experienced its true beauty and serenity. START: **Hana. Trip length: only 12 miles (19km), but at least 2 or 3 days.**

Travel Tip

Try to see Hana's attractions, especially the pools, ponds, and waterfalls, early in the day. You'll have them all to yourself. The day tourists arrive in Hana around 11am and stay until about 4pm; during that window, the area is overrun with hundreds and hundreds of people, all in a hurry, and all wanting to pack Hana's sights into just a few hours.

From Hwy. 360 turn toward the ocean on Ulaino Road, just past MM 31. The drive takes about 5 minutes.

1 ★★ kids **Kahanu Garden.** Plan to arrive when the gates open at 10am to have plenty of time to explore this 472-acre (191ha) garden, including the largest known collection of breadfruit trees in the world. The real draw here is the huge **Piilanihale Heiau** (house of Piilani), temple to one of Maui's greatest chiefs.

Torch Ginger at Kahanu Garden.

Believed to be the largest temple in the state, this structure's mammoth proportions—340 feet×415 feet (104m×126m), with walls 50 feet (15m) tall and 8 to 10 feet (2.4m–3m) thick—are humbling. Historians believe that Piilani's two sons and his grandson built the enormous temple, which was dedicated to war, sometime in the 1500s. ⏱ *1 hr. Ulaino Rd.* ☎ *808/248-8912. www.ntbg.org. Guided tours $25; self-guided tours $10; children 12 and under free. Mon–Fri 10am–2pm.*

Go back to Hwy. 360 and turn left, just past MM 32, turn left, take the road to the ocean.

2 ★★★ kids **Waianapanapa State Park.** Get up early to see shiny black-sand Waianapanapa Beach and hike the coastal trail. Plan to spend at least a couple of hours at this 120-acre (49ha) park that appears like a vivid dream, with bright-green jungle foliage on three sides and cobalt-blue water lapping at its shore. Swimming is not the best here (rough

The black sand at Waianapanapa Beach.

seas, strong currents), but you can hike a trail (p 80) along the ancient lava flow that passes by sea cliffs, lava tubes, arches, and the beach. *End of Waianapanapa Rd. off Hana Hwy. (Hwy. 360), Hana. ☎ 808/248-4843. Open daily 24 hours.*

Continue on Hwy. 360. As you enter Hana, the road splits about ½ mile (.8km) past MM 33, at the police station. Both roads will take you to Hana, but Uakea Road is more scenic.

3 ★ kids Hana Cultural Center and Museum. With the sun starting to reach its zenith, take a cooling break while touring this small museum's excellent collection of Hawaiian quilts, artifacts, books, and photos. Kids will love the **Kauhala O Hana,** consisting of four *hale* (houses) for living, meeting, cooking, and canoe building or canoe storage. ⏱ *30 min. 4974 Uakea Rd. ☎ 808/248-8622. http://hookele.com/hccm. Daily 10am–4pm.*

Turn toward the mountains at Keawa Place, then go left on Hwy. 360 for a ½ mile (.8km).

4 Hasegawa General Store. Time for lunch. Hana doesn't have a lot of culinary options (and the few that exist are either very expensive, or not that appetizing). I usually head for this legendary general store, established in 1910 and immortalized in song since 1961, to find some picnic items (chips, fruit, cookies, soda, bread, lunch fixings). The aisles are choked with merchandise: organic dried fruit, every type of soda and juice you can imagine, a variety of breads and lunch meats, baby food, napkins, and other necessities. You could spend a good 20 minutes just marveling at all of the products they cram into this tiny space. Then head to Hana Bay for a picnic. *Hwy. 360, Hana. ☎ 808/248-8231. $.*

Trace your route back to Uakea Road, turn right to the bay. It's less than ½ mile (.8km).

5 ★ kids Hana Bay. You'll find restrooms, showers, picnic tables, barbecue areas, and even a snack bar (which I would pass up—it's expensive and not the best cuisine on Maui). Enjoy watching the activities in the bay—fishermen, surfers, swimmers, and beachcombers—as you eat your lunch. Then take a short, 5- to 10-minute after-lunch hike. Look for the 386-foot (118km), red-face cinder cone beside the bay. This is **Kauiki Hill,** site of numerous fierce battles in ancient Hawaii and the birthplace of Queen Kaahumanu in 1768, who played a huge roll in Hawaii's history by encouraging her people to convert from the old religion to Christianity. A leisurely stroll will take you to her birthplace. Look for the trail along the hill on the wharf side, and follow the path through the ironwood trees; the lighthouse on the point will come into view, and you'll see pocket beaches of red cinder below. Honeymooners might want to picnic in this romantic secluded spot.

Cross Uakea Road, and drive up Keawa Place; turn left on Hwy. 360. It's less than ½ mile (.8km).

6 Hotel Hana-Maui. If you can afford it, this is THE place to stay in Hana (and one of the state's top resorts). If they aren't too busy, the staff generally is amenable to taking you on a tour in their speedy golf carts. They have an elegant spa here, too. Plan on a half-hour to see this elegant resort, longer if you want to get a meal or a drink at one of the restaurants here. See p 113.

On the green hills above Hotel Hana-Maui:

7 kids Fagan's Cross. If you have a carload of kids and don't think they'd settle down long enough to tour the Hotel Hana-Maui, then take them for a hike up this hill to the 30-foot-high (9m) white cross (made of lava rock), erected in memory of Paul Fagan, who founded the Hana Ranch as well as the Hotel Hana-Maui. The 3-mile (4.8km), round-trip hike provides a gorgeous view of the Hana coast, especially at sunset. The uphill trail starts across Hana Highway from the Hotel Hana-Maui. (Enter the pastures at your own risk; they're often occupied by glaring bulls and cows with new calves.) Watch your step as you ascend this steep hill. The hike can take 1 to 2 hours, depending on how fast you hike and how long you linger at the top admiring the breathtaking view.

Back on Hwy. 30, just past Hauoli Road about ¼ mile (.4km):

8 Wananalua Congregation Church. Stop in and see this historic church, built from coral stones from 1838 to 1842 during the missionary rush to convert the natives.

But be aware: Hawaiians whisper among themselves that it was built atop an old Hawaiian *heiau* (temple), considered not very politically correct today. ⏱ *15 min. Hwy. 30, just past Hauoli Rd.*

Just past the church, on the right side of Hwy. 30:

9 Hana Ranch Center. This small cluster of one-story buildings is Hana's commercial center, with a post office, bank, general store, the Hana Ranch Stables, and a restaurant and snack bar. If you are hungry or thirsty they can help you out here. *Hwy. 30.*

Continue past Hana on Hwy. 31 for 8 miles (13km).

10 ★★★ kids Oheo Gulch. Time to hit the water again. This is the Kipahulu end of Haleakala National Park. For years people called this series of stair-step waterfalls and pools "Seven Sacred Pools." There are more than 7 pools—about 24, actually—and all water in Hawaii is considered sacred. Don't miss my favorite spot, magnificent 400-foot (122m) **Waimoku Falls,** reachable

Wananalua Church with Fagan's Cross in the background.

Waimoku Falls.

via an often-muddy, but rewarding, hourlong uphill hike. The Kipahulu rangers offer safety information, exhibits, books, and a variety of walks and hikes year-round; check at the station for current activities. Expect showers on the Kipahulu coast. ☎ 808/248-7375. www.nps.gov/hale. Admission $5 per person or $10 per car.

Continue a mile past Oheo Gulch on the ocean side of Hwy. 31.

⓫ **Lindbergh's Grave.** Visitors of a certain generation—as well as those interested in the history of aviation—make the trek to honor renowned aviator Charles A. Lindbergh (1902–74), who was the first to fly across the Atlantic. He settled in Kipahulu, where he died of cancer in 1974, and was buried under river stones in a seaside graveyard behind the 1857 **Palapala Hoomau**

Congregational Church. You'll have no trouble finding his tombstone, which is engraved with his favorite words from the 139th Psalm: "If I take the wings of the morning and dwell in the uttermost parts of the sea."

About 5 miles (8km) farther down on Hwy. 31:

⓬ **Kaupo.** If you still have daylight, you can continue on (or you can wait until the next day) to the highlights of remote, rural Kaupo. These include the restored 1859 **Huialoha Congregationalist "Circuit" Church,** where the view of the ocean is the main attraction; and farther down the road, the **Kaupo Store,** an eclectic old country store that carries a range of bizarre goods and doesn't keep any of its posted hours, but is a fun place to "talk story" with the staff about this area, which at one time had quite a population. Store: ☎ 808/248-8054. Mon–Fri 7:30am–4:30pm. ●

Oheo Gulch.

Beaches Best Bets

Best **Black Sand**
★ Waianapanapa State Park, *MM 32, Hana Highway (Hwy. 360), Hana (p 80)*

Best for **Body Surfing**
★ H. P. Baldwin Park, *MM 6, Hana Highway (Hwy. 360), between Spreckelsville and Paia (p 77)*; and ★★ Hamoa Beach, *Haneoo Road, Hana (p 76)*

Best for **Solitude**
★★ D. T. Fleming Beach Park, *Honoapiilani Highway (Hwy. 30), Kapalua (p 76)*

Best for **Families**
★ Kamaole III Beach Park, *South Kihei Road, Kihei (p 77)*

Best for **Hawaiian History & Culture**
★ Waianapanapa State Park, *MM 32, Hana Highway (Hwy. 360), Hana (p 80)*

Longest **White-Sand Beach**
★★ Oneloa Beach (Big Beach), *South Makena Road, Makena (p 78)*

Best for **Kayaking**
★★ Maluaka Beach (Makena Beach), *Makena Road, Makena (p 78)*; and ★★★ Kapalua Beach, *past MM 30 by Napali Kai Beach Resort, Honoapiilani Road, Kapalua (p 77)*

Best for **Picnicking**
Wahikuli County Wayside Park, *MM 23, Honoapiilani Highway (Hwy. 30), Lahaina (p 79)*

Best **Protected Beach**
★★★ Kapalua Beach, *past MM 30, by Napali Kai Beach Resort, Honoapiilani Road, Kapalua (p 77)*

Most **Romantic**
★★ Wailea Beach, *fronting Four Seasons Maui and the Grand Wailea Resort, Wailea Alanui Road, Wailea (p 80)*

Best for **People-Watching**
★★ Kaanapali Beach, *Kaanapali (p 77)*

Safest for **Kids**
Launiupoko County Wayside Park, *MM 18, Honoapiilani Highway (Hwy. 30), Lahaina (p 78)*

Safest for **Swimming**
★ Kamaole III Beach Park, *South Kihei Road, Kihei (p 77)*

Best for **Shade**
★★ D. T. Fleming Beach Park, *Honoapiilani Highway (Hwy. 30), Kapalua (p 76)*

Best for **Snorkeling**
★★ Kaanapali Beach, *fronting Sheraton Maui, Kaanapali (p 77)*

Best for **Board Surfing**
★★ Hamoa Beach, *Haneoo Road, Hana (p 76)*

Best **View**
★★ Maluaka Beach (Makena Beach), *Makena Road, Makena (p 78)*

Best for **Windsurfing**
★ Hookipa Beach Park, *MM 9, Hana Highway (Hwy. 36), Paia (p 76)*

Best for **Sunbathing**
★★ Hamoa Beach, *Haneoo Road, Hana (p 76)*

Baldwin Beach.

Maui Beaches A to Z

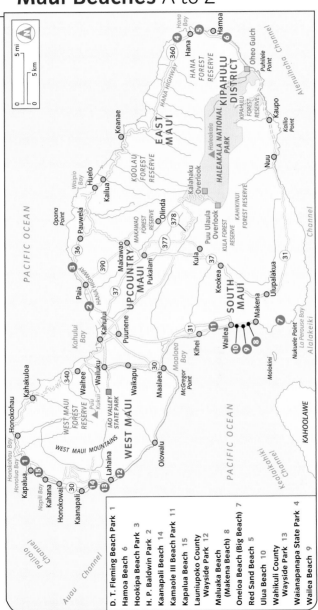

D. T. Fleming Beach Park 1
Hamoa Beach 6
Hookipa Beach Park 3
H. P. Baldwin Park 2
Kaanapali Beach 14
Kamaole III Beach Park 11
Kapalua Beach 15
Launiupoko County
   Wayside Park 12
Maluaka Beach
   (Makena Beach) 8
Oneloa Beach (Big Beach) 7
Red Sand Beach 5
Ulua Beach 10
Wahikuli County
   Wayside Park 13
Waianapanapa State Park 4
Wailea Beach 9

Photo p 73: Empty hammock on beach in Maui.

★★ kids D. T. Fleming Beach Park. This quiet, out-of-the-way beach cove is a great place to take the family. The crescent-shaped beach, north of the Ritz-Carlton Hotel, is bordered by ironwood trees, which provide shade on the land side. The water is generally good for swimming and snorkeling. Facilities include restrooms, showers, picnic tables, barbecue grills, and a paved parking lot. *Past MM 30, Honoapiilani Hwy. (Hwy. 30), Kapalua.*

★★ Hamoa Beach. This half-moon-shaped, gray-sand beach (a mix of coral and lava) in a truly tropical setting is a favorite among sunbathers seeking rest and refuge. The Hotel Hana-Maui maintains the beach and acts as if it's private, which it isn't—so just march down the lava-rock steps and grab a spot on the sand. The 100-foot-wide (30m) beach is three football fields long and sits below 30-foot (9.1m) black-lava sea cliffs. Hamoa is often swept by powerful rip currents. Surf breaks offshore and rolls ashore, making this a popular surfing and bodysurfing area. The calm left side is best for snorkeling in summer. The hotel has numerous facilities for guests; an outdoor shower and restrooms are available to nonguests.

Hamoa's gray-sand beach.

Parking is limited. *Haneoo Rd., off Hana Hwy. (Hwy. 360), Hana.*

★ Hookipa Beach Park. Due to its constant winds and endless waves, Hookipa attracts top windsurfers and wave jumpers from around the globe. Surfers and fishermen also enjoy this small, gold-sand beach at the foot of a grassy cliff, which provides a natural amphitheater for spectators. Except when international competitions are being held, weekdays are the best time to watch the daredevils fly over the waves. When the water is flat, snorkelers and divers explore the reef. Facilities include restrooms,

Maui's Beautiful Beaches

Maui has more than 80 accessible beaches of every conceivable description, from rocky black-sand beauties to powdery golden ones. The ones I've described in this chapter represent my personal favorites, carefully chosen to suit a variety of needs, tastes, and interests. All beaches (even those in front of exclusive resorts) are public property, and you are welcome to visit. Hawaii state law requires all resorts and hotels to offer public right-of-way access to the beach, along with public parking. So don't be shy—just because a beach fronts a hotel doesn't mean that you can't enjoy the water.

showers, pavilions, picnic tables, barbecue grills, and a parking lot. *2 miles past Paia, just before MM 9, Hana Hwy. (Hwy. 36), Paia.*

H. P. Baldwin Park. This beach park draws lots of Maui residents, especially body-board enthusiasts. The surf breaks along the entire length of the white sand, creating perfect conditions for body boarding. On occasion the waves get big enough for surfing. A couple of swimming areas are safe enough for children: one in the lee of the beach rocks near the large pavilion, and another at the opposite end of the beach, where beach rocks create a small protected area. Facilities include a large pavilion with picnic tables and kitchen facilities, barbecue grills, additional picnic tables on the grassy area, restrooms, showers, a semipaved parking area, a baseball diamond, and a soccer field. The park is busy on weekends; weekdays are much quieter. *At MM 6, Hana Hwy. (Hwy. 360), btw. Spreckelsville and Paia, turn left on Alawai Rd. follow to the ocean.*

★★ Kaanapali Beach. Four-mile-long (6.4km) Kaanapali is one of Maui's best beaches, with grainy gold sand as far as the eye can see. Because Kaanapali is so long, and because most hotels have adjacent swimming pools, the beach is crowded only in pockets—you'll find plenty of spots to be alone. Summertime swimming is excellent. There's fabulous snorkeling around **Black Rock,** in front of the Sheraton. The water is clear, calm, and populated with clouds of tropical fish. You might even spot a turtle or two. Facilities consist of outdoor showers. Parking is a problem, though. *Look for* PUBLIC BEACH ACCESS *signs off Kaanapali Pkwy., off Honoapiilani Hwy. (Hwy. 30), at the Kaanapali Resort.*

★ kids Kamaole III Beach Park. On weekends this beach is jampacked with fishermen, picnickers, swimmers, and snorkelers. But during the week "Kam-3," as locals call it, is often empty. This beach park features a playground for children and a grassy lawn that meets the sand. Swimming is safe, but scattered lava rocks are toe stubbers at the water line, and parents should watch to make sure that kids don't venture too far out, because the bottom slopes off quickly. Both the north and south shores are rocky fingers with a surge big enough to attract fish (and snorkelers to watch them), while winter waves attract bodysurfers. Facilities include restrooms, showers, picnic tables, barbecue grills, and lifeguards. *S. Kihei Rd., across from Keonekai Rd., Kihei.*

★★★ Kapalua Beach. This is a postcard-perfect beach: a golden crescent bordered by two palm-studded points. Protected from strong winds and currents by lava-rock promontories, Kapalua's calm waters are great for snorkelers and swimmers of all ages and abilities, and the bay is big enough to paddle a kayak around without getting into the more challenging channel that

Kamaole III Beach Park.

Kapalua Beach.

separates Maui from Molokai. Fish hang out by the rocks, making it great for snorkeling. Facilities include outdoor showers, restrooms, lifeguards, a rental shack, and plenty of shade. Parking is limited to about 30 spaces in a small lot. *Past MM 30, by Napali Kai Beach Resort, Honoapiilani Rd., Kapalua.*

kids Launiupoko County Wayside Park. Families with children will love this small, shady park with a large wading pool for kids and a small sandy beach with good swimming when conditions are right. The view from the park is one of the best, with the islands of Kahoolawe, Lanai, and Molokai in the distance. Facilities include a paved parking lot, restrooms, showers, picnic tables, and barbecue grills. It's crowded on weekends. *MM 18, Honoapiilani Hwy. (Hwy. 30), Lahaina.*

★★ Maluaka Beach (Makena Beach). This is the place for views: Molokini Crater and Kahoolawe are both visible in the distance. Maluaka itself is a short, wide, palm-fringed crescent of golden, grainy sand set between two black-lava points and bounded by big sand dunes topped by a grassy knoll. Swimming and kayaking in the mostly calm bay are first-rate. Facilities include restrooms, showers, a landscaped park, lifeguards, and roadside parking. *Along Makena Alanui, look for the shoreline access sign near the Makena Prince Hotel, turn right, and head down to the shore on Makena Rd., Makena.*

★★ Oneloa Beach (Big Beach). Oneloa (Long Sand), known as Big Beach, is 3,300 feet (1,006m) long and more than 100 feet (30m) wide. Mauians come here to swim, fish, sunbathe, surf, and enjoy the view of Kahoolawe and Lanai. Snorkeling is good around the north end at the foot of Puu Olai, a 360-foot (110m)

Maluaka Beach.

cinder cone. During storms, however, big waves lash the shore and a strong rip current sweeps the sharp drop-off, posing a danger for inexperienced open-ocean swimmers. On the other side of Puu Olai is **Little Beach,** a small pocket beach where assorted nudists work on their all-over tans (much to the chagrin of uptight authorities, who take a dim view of public nudity). You could get a sunburn in a sensitive spot and a lewd-conduct ticket, too. Facilities include portable toilets and parking. *South Makena Rd., Makena.*

Red Sand Beach. This beach on the ocean side of Kauiki Hill, just south of Hana Bay, is truly a sight to see. It's in a wild, natural setting on a pocket cove, where the volcanic cinder cone lost its seaward wall to erosion and spilled red cinders everywhere, creating the red sands. But before you put on your bathing suit, there are three things to know about this beach: You have to trespass to get here (which is against the law); it can be extremely dangerous due to heavy rains (there have been several serious injuries on the muddy, slippery terrain); and nudity (also illegal in Hawaii) is common here. If you are determined to go, ask for permission at the Hotel Hana-Maui. Also inquire about conditions on the trail (which drops several stories down to the ocean rocks). To reach the beach, put on solid walking shoes (no flip-flops) and walk south on Uakea Road, past Haoli Street and the Hotel Hana-Maui, to the parking lot for the hotel's Sea Ranch Cottages. Turn left and cross the open field next to the Hana Community Center. Look for the dirt trail and follow it to the huge ironwood tree, where you turn right (do not go ahead to the old Japanese cemetery). Use the ironwood trees to maintain your balance as you follow the ever-eroding

Oneloa Beach.

cinder footpath a short distance along the shoreline, down the narrow cliff trail (do not attempt this if it's wet). The trail suddenly turns a corner, and into view comes the burnt-red beach, set off by the turquoise waters, black lava, and vivid green ironwood trees. The lava outcropping protects the bay and makes it safe for swimming. Snorkeling is excellent, and there's a natural whirlpool area on the Hana Bay side of the cove. Stay away from the surge area where the ocean enters the cove.

★ **Ulua Beach.** One of the most popular beaches in Wailea, Ulua is a long, wide, crescent-shaped gold-sand beach between two rocky points. When the ocean is calm, Ulua offers Wailea's best snorkeling; when it's rough, the waves are excellent for bodysurfers. Crowded conditions make it perfect for meeting people. Facilities include showers and restrooms. *Look for the blue shoreline access sign, on Wailea Alanui Dr., Wailea.*

Wahikuli County Wayside Park. This small stretch of beach is

The Best Beaches

Wailea Beach.

★ **Waianapanapa State Park.** This 120-acre (49ha) beach park is a wonderful area for both shoreline hikes (mosquitoes are plentiful, so bring insect repellent) and picnicking. Swimming is generally unsafe due to powerful rip currents and strong waves breaking offshore, which roll into the black-sand beach unchecked. Waianapanapa is crowded on weekends; weekdays are generally a better bet. Facilities include 12 cabins, a beach park, picnic tables, barbecue grills, restrooms, showers, and a parking lot. *MM 32, Hana Hwy. (Hwy. 360), Hana. See p 89.*

★★ **Wailea Beach.** From this beach, the view out to sea is magnificent, framed by neighboring Kahoolawe and Lanai and the tiny crescent of Molokini. Grab your sweetie at sunset and watch the clear waters tumble to shore; this is as romantic as it gets. Facilities include restrooms, outdoor showers, and limited free parking. *Look for the blue shoreline access sign, on Wailea Alanui Dr., Wailea.* ●

one of Lahaina's most popular beach parks. It's packed on weekends, but during the week it's a great place for swimming, snorkeling, sunbathing, and picnics. Facilities include paved parking, restrooms, showers, and small covered pavilions with picnic tables and barbecue grills. *MM 23, Honoapiilani Hwy. (Hwy. 30), btw. Lahaina and Kaanapali.*

The Legend of Waianapanapa

Waianapanapa Park gets its name from the legend of the Waianapanapa Cave. Chief Kaakea, a jealous and cruel man, suspected his wife, Popoalaea, of having an affair. Popoalaea left her husband and hid herself in a chamber of the Waianapanapa Cave. A few days later, when Kaakea was passing by the cave, the shadow of a servant gave away Popoalaea's hiding place, and Kaakea killed her. During certain times of the year, the water in the tide pool turns red as a tribute to Popoalaea, commemorating her death. (Killjoy scientists claim, however, that the change in color is due to the presence of small red shrimp.)

Haleakala National Park

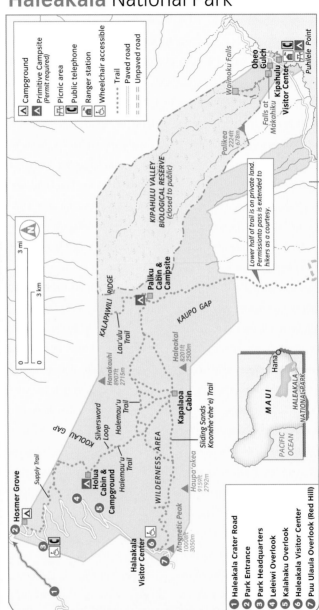

Campground
Primitive Campsite *(Permit required)*
Picnic area
Public telephone
Ranger station
Wheelchair accessible

.... Trail
——— Paved road
= = = = Unpaved road

Waimoku Falls

Oheo Gulch

Puhilele Point

Falls at Makahiku

Kipahulu Visitor Center

KIPAHULU VALLEY BIOLOGICAL RESERVE (closed to public)

Palikea 2224ft 678m

Lower half of trail is on private land. Permission to cross is extended to hikers as a courtesy.

KALAPAWILI RIDGE

Paliku Cabin & Campsite

KAUPO GAP

Lau'ulu Trail

Haleakal 8201ft 2500m

Hanakauhi 8907ft 2715m

Halemau'u Trail

Silversword Loop

KOOLAU GAP

Kapalaoa Cabin

Sliding Sands Keonehe'ehe'e) Trail

Haupa'akea 9159ft 2792m

WILDERNESS AREA

Supply Trail

Hosmer Grove

Holua Cabin & Campground

Halemau'u Trail

Magnetic Peak 10008ft 3050m

Haleakala Visitor Center

MAUI

Hana

HALEAKALA NATIONAL PARK

PACIFIC OCEAN

1 Haleakala Crater Road
2 Park Entrance
3 Park Headquarters
4 Leleiwi Overlook
5 Kalahaku Overlook
6 Haleakala Visitor Center
7 Puu Ulaula Overlook (Red Hill)

3 mi

3 km

Previous page: A surfer drops to the curl of Hawaii's big surf at Peahi Jaws.

At once forbidding and compelling, Haleakala (house of the sun) National Park is Maui's most compelling natural attraction. More than 1.3 million people a year ascend the 10,023-foot-high (3,055m) mountain to peer into the crater of the world's largest dormant volcano. The crater is large enough that the entire island of Manhattan would fit inside: 3,000 feet (914m) deep, 7½ miles (12km) long, 2½ miles (4km) wide, and encompassing 19 square miles (49 sq. km). But there's more to do here than simply stare in a big black hole: Just going up the mountain is an experience in itself. The snaky road passes through big, puffy, cumulus clouds, climbing from sea level to 10,000 feet (3,048m) in just 37 miles (60km) to offer magnificent views of the isthmus of Maui, the West Maui Mountains, and the Pacific Ocean. START: **Kahului. Trip length: 37 miles (60km); about a 2-hour drive.**

Travel Tip

Pukalani is the last town for water, food, and gas (there are no facilities beyond the ranger stations). On the way back down, put your car in low gear so you won't destroy your brakes on the descent.

From Kahului, take Hwy. 37 to Hwy. 377 to Hwy. 378.

1 ★★★ **Haleakala Crater Road.** If you look on a Maui map, there's a black wiggly line that looks like this: WWWWW. That's Hwy. 378, also known as Haleakala Crater Road—one of the fastest-ascending roads in the world. This grand corniche has at least 33 switchbacks; passes through numerous climate zones; goes under, in, and out of clouds; takes you past rare silversword plants and endangered Hawaiian geese sailing through the clear, thin air; and offers a view that extends for more than 100 miles (161km). Along the way, expect fog, rain, and wind. You might also encounter stray cattle and downhill bicyclists.

2 **Park Entrance.** A ranger will collect the entrance fee of $10 per car (or $2 for a bicycle), good for a week of unlimited entry.

3 **Park Headquarters.** Here you can pick up information on park programs and activities and get camping permits. Restrooms, a pay phone, and drinking water are available. Don't miss my favorite Haleakala native, Hawaii's endangered **nene,** or Hawaiian goose. With its black face, buff cheeks, and partially webbed feet, the gray-brown bird looks like a small Canada goose with zebra stripes; it brays out "nay-nay" (hence its name), doesn't migrate, and prefers lava beds to lakes. The unusual goose clings to a precarious existence on these

Hawaii's endangered nene.

Before You Go

At the 10,023-foot (3,055m) summit of Haleakala National Park, weather changes fast. With wind chill, temperatures can drop below freezing any time of year. Summers are usually dry and warm; winters wet, windy, and cold. Before you go, get current weather conditions from the park (☎ 808/572-4400) or the **National Weather Service** (☎ 808/871-5054). Bring water and a jacket or a blanket, especially if you go up for sunrise. (Sunsets at the summit are also spectacular.)

As you ascend the slopes, the temperature drops about 3 degrees every 1,000 feet (305m), so the top can be 30 degrees cooler than it was at sea level. Come prepared with sweaters, jackets, and rain gear.

From sunrise to noon, the light is weak, but the view is usually cloud free. The best time for photos is in the afternoon, when the sun lights the crater and clouds are sparse. Full-moon nights also make for spectacular viewing.

alpine slopes. Vast populations of more than 25,000 once inhabited Hawaii, but predation coupled with habitat destruction have nearly caused its extinction. By 1951, there were only 30 left. Now protected as Hawaii's state bird, the wild nene on Haleakala number fewer than 250. ☎ *808/572-4400. www.nps.gov/ hale. Daily 7am–4pm.*

④ ★ **Leleiwi Overlook.** Just beyond MM 17, pull into the parking area. From here a short trail leads

Bikers admiring the view from Kalahaku Overlook.

A rare silversword.

you to a panoramic view of the lunarlike crater. When the clouds are low and the sun is in the right place, usually around sunset, you can experience a phenomenon known as the "Specter of the Brocken"—you can see a reflection of your shadow, ringed by a rainbow, in the clouds below. It's an optical illusion caused by a rare combination of sun, shadow, and fog that occurs only three places on the planet: Haleakala, Scotland, and Germany.

⑤ ★ Kalahaku Overlook. This is the best place to see a rare **silversword.** Looking like something from outer space, its silvery bayonets display tiny purple bouquets—like a spacey artichoke with attitude. This botanical wonder proved irresistible to collectors, who gathered them in gunnysacks for Chinese potions, for British specimen collections, and just for the sheer thrill of

having something so unusual. Silverswords grow only in Hawaii, take from 4 to 50 years to bloom, and then, usually between May and October, send up a 1- to 6-foot (.3–1.8m) stalk with a purple bouquet of sunflower-like blooms.

⑥ ★ Haleakala Visitor Center. Just before the summit, this small building offers a panoramic view of the volcanic landscape, with photos identifying the various features and exhibits that explain its history, ecology, geology, and volcanology. Park staff is often on hand to answer questions. The only facilities are restrooms and water. Rangers offer excellent, informative, and free **naturalist talks** at 9:30, 10:30, and 11:30am daily in the summit building and lead guided hikes from here. *Near the summit, 11 miles (18km) from the park entrance. P.O. Box 369, Makawao, HI 96768. ☎ 808/572-4400. www.nps.gov/hale. Daily sunrise–3pm.*

⑦ ★★ Puu Ulaula Overlook (Red Hill). This is it, the volcano's highest point—you'll feel as if you're at the edge of the earth. You'll also notice a mysterious cluster of buildings officially known as Haleakala Observatories, but unofficially called **Science City.** If you're here at sunrise, the building at Puu Ulaula Overlook, a triangle of glass that serves as a windbreak, is the best viewing spot. After the daily miracle of sunrise—the sun seems to rise out of the vast crater (hence the name Haleakala, which means "house of the sun")—you can see all the way across Alenuihaha Channel to the often snowcapped summit of Mauna Kea on the Big Island.

The Great Outdoors

Maui's Best Hiking & Camping

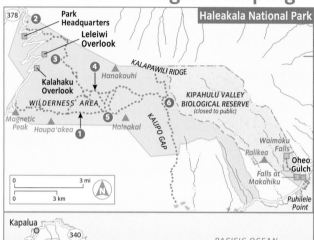

Haleakala National Park

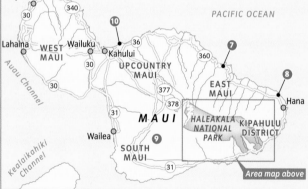

Hiking

Haleakala National Park: Halemauu Trail 4
Haleakala National Park: Sliding Sands Trail 1
Keanae Arboretum 7
Polipoli State Park 9
Waianapanapa State Park 8

Camping

Haleakala National Park: Holua 3
Haleakala National Park: Hosmer Grove 2
Haleakala National Park: Paliku 6
Kanaha Beach Park 10
Polipoli State Park 9
Waianapanapa State Park 8

Cabin Camping
in Haleakala National Park

Holua 3
Kapalaoa 5
Paliku 6

In the past 3 decades, Maui has grown from a rural island to a fast-paced resort destination, but its natural beauty largely remains; there are still many places that can be explored only on foot. Bring your own gear, as there are no places to rent camping equipment on Maui.

Haleakala National Park

★★★ **Hiking.** Hiking into Maui's dormant volcano is the best way to see it. The terrain inside the wilderness area of the volcano, which ranges from burnt-red cinder cones to ebony-black lava flows, is simply spectacular. Inside the crater are some 27 miles (43km) of hiking trails, two camping sites, and three cabins. The best route takes in two trails: You head into the crater along Sliding Sands Trail, which begins on the rim at 9,800 feet (2,987m) and descends to the valley floor at 6,600 feet (2,012m), and back out along Halemauu Trail. The 11-mile (18km) one-way descent takes 9 hours. For more information on visiting Haleakala, see p 82. *To get to the summit from Kahului, take Hwy. 37 to Hwy. 377 to Hwy. 378.* ☎ *808/572-4400. www.nps.gov/hale.*

Camping. Hosmer Grove, at 6,800 feet (2,073m), is a small, open grassy area surrounded by a forest near the entrance to Haleakala National Park. This is the best place to spend the night in a tent if you want to see the Haleakala sunrise. No permits are needed at Hosmer Grove, and there's no charge—but you can stay for only 3 nights (just 2 of those consecutive) during a 30-day period. The two tent-camping areas inside the volcano are **Holua,** just off Halemauu at 6,920 feet (2,109m); and **Paliku,** just before the Kaupo Gap at the eastern end of the valley, at 6,380 feet (1,945m). Facilities at both campgrounds are limited to pit toilets and nonpotable catchment water. Permits are issued daily at park headquarters on a first-come, first-served basis.

Cabin Camping. The three cabins inside the crater are spaced so that each is an easy walk from the previous one: **Holua** cabin is on the Halemauu Trail, **Kapalaoa** cabin is on the Sliding Sands Trail, and **Paliku** cabin is on the eastern end by the **Kaupo Gap.** The cabin here has 12 padded bunks (but no bedding; bring your o`wn), a table, chairs, cooking utensils, a two-burner propane stove, and a

Hiking in Haleakala.

Getting a Camping Permit

All campers on Maui must have a permit. The requirements vary, and it does take time and effort to get a permit. Depending on where you're headed (see write-ups below), the following places issue permits: **Haleakala National Park** (P.O. Box 369, Makawao, HI 96768; ☎ 808/572-4400; www.nps.gov/hale), **Hawaii State Department of Land and Natural Resources,** State Parks Division (P.O. Box 621, Honolulu, HI 96809; ☎ 808/587-0300; www.hawaiistate parks.org/camping/fees.cfm), and **Maui County Parks and Recreation** (1580-C Kaahumanu Ave., Wailuku, HI 96793; ☎ 808/243-7380; www.mauimapp.com/information/campingcounty.htm). Fees are $5 per campsite per night in Hawaii state parks. Fees for Maui County camping are $5 for adults and $2 for children ages 17 and under Monday to Thursday. Friday to Sunday stays are more expensive, with fees increased to $8 for adults and $3 for children.

wood-burning stove with firewood (you might also have a few cockroaches). When reserved within 3 weeks of your stay, the fee is nonrefundable and the reservation cannot be changed. A flat rate for 1 to 12 people is $60 for the entire cabin if reserved less than 3 weeks ahead. Call between 1 and 3pm Hawaii Standard Time any day to find out these restricted last-minute availabilities or for more information, call ☎ 808/572-4459. You will need a valid credit card to secure a reservation by phone. The cabins are so popular that the National Park Service has a lottery system for reservations. You're limited to no more than 2 nights in one cabin and no more than 3 nights within the wilderness per month.

Kanaha Beach Park
Camping. This popular county park has two separate areas for camping: 7 tent sites on the beach and an additional 10 tent sites inland. The park is a favorite of windsurfers, who take advantage of the strong winds that roar across this end of the island. Facilities include a paved parking lot, portable toilets, outdoor showers, barbecue grills, and picnic tables. Camping is limited to 3 consecutive days; the park is closed to camping on Monday and Tuesday. *Alahao St. in Kahalui, just west of the Kahului Airport.*

Keanae Arboretum
Hiking. This easy 2-mile (3.2km), family-friendly walk through the Keanae Arboretum, passes through a forest with both native and introduced plants. Allow 1 to 2 hours, longer if you want to swim. Bring rain gear and mosquito repellent. *47 miles (76km) from Kahului, along the Hana Hwy.*

Polipoli State Park
★ **Hiking & Camping.** At 5,300 to 6,200 feet (1,615m–1,890m), and part of the 21,000-acre (8,498ha) Kula and Kahikinui Forest Reserve on the slope of Haleakala, Polipoli doesn't seem like your typical image of Hawaii (it's downright cold at 6,200 ft./1,890m!). But there's great hiking on the Polipoli Loop, an easy, 5-mile (8km) hike that

takes about 3 hours and branches out to a variety of longer trails. Camping is allowed in the park with a $5-per-night permit from the Division of State Parks; see the box, "Getting a Camping Permit," above. *Take Hwy. 37 to Keokea and turn right on Hwy. 337; after less than ½ mile (.8km) turn on Waipoli Rd. and continue for 10 miles (16km) to the park.*

Waianapanapa State Park
★★★ Hiking & Camping.
Tucked in a tropical jungle, on the outskirts of the little coastal town of Hana, is Waianapanapa State Park, a black-sand beach set in an emerald forest, with camping and hiking. The coastal trail is an easy, 6-mile (9.7km) hike that parallels the sea, traveling past lava cliffs and a forest of *lauhala* trees. Allow 4 hours for the hike. The best time of day is either the early morning or the late evening, when the light on the lava and surf makes for great photos. The park has 12 cabins and a tent campground. Go for the cabins, as it rains torrentially here, sometimes turning the campground into something like a mud-wrestling arena.

Waianapanapa State Park.

Fees for the cabins are $45 per night for one to four people, and $5 per night for each additional person. A 50% deposit is required per cabin. Tent camping is $5 per night but limited to 5 nights in a 30-day period. Permits are available from the State Parks Division; see the box, "Getting a Camping Permit," above. *Just after MM 32, turn off the Hana Hwy. (Hwy.360) at the* WAIANAPANAPA STATE PARK *sign. Continue down Waianapanapa Rd. to the end.*

Safe Hiking & Camping

Water might be everywhere in Hawaii, but more than likely it isn't safe to drink. The Department of Health continually warns campers of *bacterium leptospirosis,* which is found in freshwater streams throughout the state and enters the body through breaks in the skin or through the mucous membranes. It produces flulike symptoms and can be fatal. Firewood isn't always available, so it's a good idea to carry a small, light, backpacking stove. Make sure that your drinking water is safe by vigorously boiling it, or use tablets with hydroperiodide; portable water filters will not screen out *bacterium leptospirosis.*

Remember, Maui is not crime free: Never leave your valuables unprotected. Carry a day pack and never camp alone.

Some more rules of thumb: Do bury personal waste away from streams, don't eat unknown fruit, do carry your trash out, and don't forget that it gets dark quickly.

Maui's Best Golf Courses

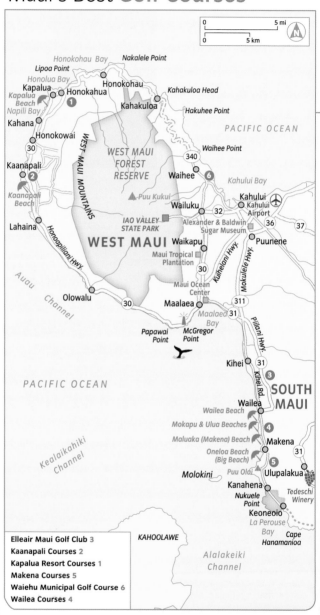

Elleair Maui Golf Club 3
Kaanapali Courses 2
Kapalua Resort Courses 1
Makena Courses 5
Waiehu Municipal Golf Course 6
Wailea Courses 4

In some circles, Maui is synonymous with golf. The island's world-famous courses start at the northern tip of the island and roll right around to Kaanapali, jumping down to Kihei and Wailea in the south. First-time Maui golfers should know that it's windy here, especially between 10am and 2pm, when winds of 10 to 15 mph (16–24kph) are the norm. Play two to three clubs up or down to compensate. I also recommend bringing extra balls—the rough is thicker here and the wind will pick your ball up and drop it in very unappealing places (like water hazards).

Renting Golf Gear

Golf Club Rentals (📞 808/665-0800; www.mauiclubrentals.com) has custom-built clubs for men, women, and juniors (right- and left-handed), which can be delivered islandwide; rates start at $25 a day.

Elleair Maui Golf Club (formerly Silversword Golf Club). Sitting in the foothills of Haleakala, just high enough to afford spectacular ocean vistas from every hole, this is a course for golfers who love the views as much as the fairways and the greens. It's very forgiving. *Just one caveat:* Go in the morning. Not only is it cooler, but more important, it's also less windy. In the afternoon the winds bluster down Haleakala with great gusto. Facilities include a clubhouse, driving range, putting green, pro shop, and lessons. *1345 Piilani Hwy. (near Lipoa St. turnoff), Kihei.* 📞 *808/874-0777. www.golf-maui.com. Greens fees $120; twilight rate $95.*

★ **Kaanapali Courses.** The courses at Kaanapali offer a challenge to all golfers, from high handicappers to near pros. The par-72, 6,305-yard **Royal Kaanapali Course** is a true Robert Trent Jones, Sr., design: an abundance of wide bunkers; several long, stretched-out tees; and the largest, most-contoured greens on Maui. The par-72, 6,250-yard **Kaanapali Kai** is an Arthur Jack Snyder design. Although shorter

than the North Course, it requires more accuracy on the narrow, hilly fairways. Facilities include a driving range, putting course, and clubhouse with dining. You'll have a better chance of getting a tee time on weekdays. *Off Hwy. 30, Kaanapali.* 📞 *808/661-3691. www.kaanapali-golf.com. Greens fees Royal Kaanapali Course $235 ($190 for resort guests), twilight rate $120; Kaanapali Kai Course $195 ($150 for resort guests), twilight rate $95. At the first stoplight in Kaanapali, turn onto Kaanapali Pkwy.; the first building on your right is the clubhouse.*

★★★ **Kapalua Resort Courses.** The views from these two championship courses are worth the greens fees alone. The par-72, 6,761-yard **Bay Course** (📞 808/669-8820) was designed by Arnold Palmer and Ed Seay. This course is a bit forgiving, with its wide fairways; the greens, however, are difficult to read. The **Plantation Course** (📞 808/669-8877), site of the Mercedes Championships, is a Ben Crenshaw and Bill Coore design. This par-73, 6,547-yard, course, set on a rolling hillside, is excellent for developing your low shots and precise chipping. Facilities include locker rooms, a driving range, and a good restaurant. Weekdays are your best bet for tee times. *Off Hwy. 30, Kapalua.* 📞 *877/KAPALUA (527-2582). www.kapaluamaui.com. Greens fees Bay Course $215 ($175 for resort guests), twilight rate $130;*

Golf Tips

If you're trying to get a tee time at a public course, keep in mind that weekdays are always better than weekends, when the locals flood the field. You'll have better luck teeing off after 9am, and afternoons generally are wide open. And, of course, book in advance, as soon as you have your travel dates.

There's generally wind—10 to 30 mph (16–48kmph) is not unusual between 10am and 2pm—so you may have to play two to three clubs up or down to compensate. Bring extra balls: The rough is thick, water hazards are everywhere, and the wind wreaks havoc with your game. On the greens, your putt will *always* break toward the ocean. Hit deeper and more aggressively in the sand because the type of sand used on most Hawaii courses is firmer and more compact than on mainland courses (lighter sand would blow away in the constant wind). And bring a camera—you'll kick yourself if you don't capture those spectacular views.

Plantation Course $295 ($200 for resort guests), twilight rate $150.

★★ **Makena Courses.** Here you'll find 36 holes of "Mr. Hawaii Golf"—Robert Trent Jones, Jr.—at his best. Add to that some spectacular views: Molokini islet looms in the background, humpback whales gambol offshore in winter, and the tropical sunsets are spectacular. The par-72, 6,876-yard **South Course** has a

Makena golf courses.

couple of holes you'll never forget. The par-72, 6,823-yard **North Course** is more difficult and more spectacular. Facilities include a clubhouse, a driving range, two putting greens, a pro shop, lockers, and lessons. Beware of weekend crowds. *On Makena Alanui Dr., just past the Maui Prince Hotel.* ☎ *808/879-3344. www.makenagolf.com. Greens fees $155–$200 ($125–$130 for resort guests), twilight rates $110–$135.*

Waiehu Municipal Golf Course. This public, oceanside, par-72 golf course is like two courses in one: The first 9 holes, built in 1930, are set along the dramatic coastline, while the back 9 holes, added in 1966, head toward the mountains. It's a fun course that probably won't challenge your handicap. The only hazard here is the wind, which can rip off the ocean and play havoc with your ball. Facilities include a snack bar, driving range, practice greens, golf-club rental, and clubhouse. Because this is a public course, the greens fees are low—but getting a tee time is tough. *2199*

One of Wailea's golf courses.

Kahookele St., Wailuku, HI 96793.
☎ *808/244-5934. www.co.maui.hi.
us/parks/maui/central/waiehugolf
course.htm. Greens fees $69 Mon–Fri,
$74 Sat–Sun and holidays. From the
Kahului Airport, turn right on the
Hana Hwy. (Hwy. 36), which becomes
Kaahumanu Ave. (Hwy. 32). Turn
right at the stoplight at the junction
of Waiehu Beach Rd. (Hwy. 340). Go
another 1½ miles (2.4km), and you'll
see the entrance on your right.*

★★ **Wailea Courses.** You can
choose among three courses at
Wailea. The **Blue Course,** a par-72,
6,758-yard course designed by
Arthur Jack Snyder and dotted with
bunkers and water hazards, is for
duffers and pros alike. A little more
difficult is the par-72, 7,078-yard
championship **Gold Course,** with

narrow fairways, several tricky dog-
leg holes, and natural hazards like
lava-rock walls. The **Emerald
Course,** which like the Gold Course
was designed by Robert Trent
Jones, Jr., is Wailea's newest, with
tropical landscaping and a player-
friendly design. With 54 holes to
play, getting a tee time is slightly
easier on weekends than at other
resorts, but weekdays are still the
best (the Emerald Course is usually
the toughest to book). Facilities
include two pro shops, restaurants,
locker rooms, and a complete golf
training facility. *Wailea Alanui Dr.
(off Wailea Iki Dr.), Wailea.* ☎ *888/
328-MAUI (6284) or 808/875-7450.
www.waileagolf.com. Greens fees
$225 ($180–$190 for resort guests),
twilight rate $135.*

Golfing on a Budget

If your heart is set on playing on a resort course, book at least
a week in advance. Ardent golfers on a budget should play in the
afternoon, when discounted twilight rates are in effect. There's no
guarantee you'll get 18 holes in, especially in winter when it's dark
by 6pm, but you'll have an opportunity to experience these world-
famous courses at half the usual fee.

For last-minute and discount tee times, call **Stand-by Golf** (☎ 888/
645-BOOK [2665] or 808/874-0600; www.stand-bygolf.com) between
7am and 9pm. Stand-by offers discounted (up to 50% off greens fees),
guaranteed tee times for same-day or next-day golfing.

Adventures **on Land**

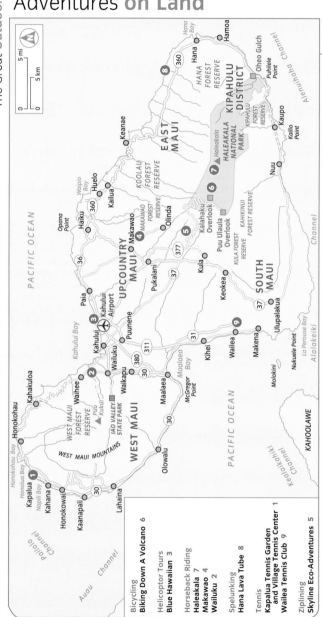

Bicycling
Biking Down A Volcano 6

Helicoptor Tours
Blue Hawaiian 3

Horseback Riding
Haleakala 7
Makawao 4
Wailuku 2

Spelunking
Hana Lava Tube 8

Tennis
Kapalua Tennis Garden
and Village Tennis Center 1
Wailea Tennis Club 9

Ziplining
Skyline Eco-Adventures 5

M aui is known for its crystal-clear waters, but you'll also discover plenty of land-based adventures to enjoy. Haleakala is perfect for bicycling and horseback riding; the warm, sunny days are terrific for tennis, and real daredevils can try ziplining.

Bicycling

Biking Down a Volcano. It's not even close to dawn, but here you are, rubbing your eyes awake, riding in a van up the long, dark road to the top of Maui's sleeping volcano. It's colder than you ever thought possible for a tropical island. The air is thin. You stomp your chilly feet while you wait, sipping hot coffee. Then comes the sun, exploding over yawning Haleakala Crater—it's a mystical moment you won't soon forget. But there's no time to linger: Decked out in your screaming yellow jacket, you mount your steed and test its most important feature, the brakes, because you're about to coast 37 miles (60km) down a 10,000-foot (3,048m) volcano. Wear layers of warm clothing—there may be a 30-degree change in temperature from the top of the mountain to the ocean. Generally, tour groups will not take riders under 12, but younger children can ride along in the van that accompanies the

groups. Pregnant women should also ride in the van. My pick for cruising down Haleakala is Maui's oldest downhill company, **Maui Downhill,** which offers a sunrise safari bike tour, including continental breakfast and brunch. All rates include hotel pickup, transport to the top, bicycle, safety equipment, and meals. *199 Dairy Rd., Kahului.* ☎ *800/535-BIKE (2453) or 808/871-2155. www.mauidownhill.com. From $125 (check website for discounts and online specials).*

Helicopter Flights

★★★ **Maui from the Air.** Only a helicopter can bring you face-to-face with remote sites like Maui's little-known Wall of Tears, near the summit of Puu Kukui in the West Maui Mountains. You'll glide through canyons etched with 1,000-foot (305m) waterfalls and over dense rainforests; you'll climb to 10,000 feet (3,048m), high enough to glimpse the summit of Haleakala,

Biking on Haleakala.

and fly by the dramatic vistas at Molokai. **Blue Hawaiian's** pilots are part Hawaiian historian, part DJ, part tour guide, and part amusement-ride operator. As you soar through the clouds, you'll learn about the island's flora, fauna, history, and culture. Blue Hawaiian is also the only helicopter company in the state to have the latest, high-tech, environmentally friendly (and quiet) Eco-Star helicopter. *Kahului Airport.* ☎ *800/745-BLUE (2583) or 808/ 871-8844. www.bluehawaiian.com. Flights vary 30–100 min. for $139– $462 per person per ride.*

Horseback Riding

Haleakala. If you'd like to ride down into Haleakala's crater, contact **Pony Express Tours,** which offers a variety of rides down to the crater floor and back up, and shorter 1- and 2-hour rides at Haleakala Ranch. *Hwy. 378, Kula.* ☎ *808/ 667-2200 or 808/878-6698. www. ponyexpresstours.com. Crater rides from $182.*

Makawao. Maui has spectacular adventure rides through rugged ranch lands, into tropical forests, and to remote swimming holes. My favorite is **Piiholo Ranch,** in Makawao. A working cattle ranch, owned by the *kamaaina* (longtime resident) Baldwin family, this is a horseback-riding adventure with a variety of rides to suit different abilities, from the morning picnic ride, a 3½-hour ride on the ranch, with a picnic lunch; to private rides, including working with the cowboys to round up the cattle. *Waiahiwi Rd., Makawao.* ☎ *866/572-5544 or 808/357-5544. www.piiholo. com. Rides start at $120.*

Wailuku. For an "out west" type of adventure, I like **Mendes Ranch & Trail Rides.** The 300-acre (121ha) Mendes Ranch is a real working

Horseback riding in Haleakala's crater.

cowboy ranch that has all the essential elements of an earthly paradise—rainbows, waterfalls, palm trees, coral-sand beaches, lagoons, tide pools, a rainforest, and its own volcanic peak (more than a mile high). Allan Mendes, a third-generation wrangler, will take you from the edge of the rainforest out to the sea. On the way, you'll cross tree-studded meadows where Texas longhorns sit in the shade and pass a dusty corral where Allan's father, Ernest, a champion roper, may be breaking in a wild horse. Allan keeps close watch, turning often in his saddle to make sure everyone is happy. He points out flora and fauna and fields questions, but generally just lets you soak up Maui's natural splendor in golden silence. My favorite is the morning ride, which lasts 2 hours and ends with a barbecue back at the corral. *3530 Kahekili Hwy., 5 miles (8km) past Wailuku.* ☎ *808/244-7320. www.mendesranch.com. Morning or afternoon ride $110, barbeque lunch additional $20.*

Spelunking

★ **Hana Lava Tube.** Don't miss the opportunity to see how the Hawaiian Islands were made by exploring a million-year-old underground lava tube/cave. Chuck Thorne, of Maui Cave Adventures, offers a look at this unique geological feature. After more than 10 years of leading scuba tours through underwater caves around Hawaii, Chuck discovered some caves on land. When the land surrounding the largest cave on Maui went on the market in 1996, Chuck snapped it up and started his own tour company. The self-guided tours take 30 to 45 minutes. *Ulaino Rd. just north of Hana.* ☎ *808/248-7308. www.mauicave. com. Sat 10:30am–3:30pm. Admission $12 ages 6 and up.*

Tennis

★★★ **Kapalua Tennis Garden and Village Tennis Center.** Opened in 1979, the Tennis Garden has 10 Plexi-Pave courts paired in tiered clusters, with four lit for night play and surrounded by lush tropical foliage. Each set of courts is secluded in landscaped privacy with its own viewing lanai. Also available: private lessons, stroke-of-the-day clinics, drop-in clinics, and tournaments. The staff will match you up with a partner if you need one. *Kapalua Resort.* ☎ *808/669-5677. www.kapaluamaui.com. Courts $16 per person ($14 per person for resort guests).*

★★ **Wailea Tennis Club.** One of Maui's best facilities for playing the game, this resort club features 11 Plexi-Pave courts (3 nighttime courts), backboard or wall, pro shop, six USPTA pros available for lessons, and three doubles clinics a week. *131 Wailea Iki Place, Wailea.* ☎ *808/879-1958. www.wailea tennis.com. Courts $15 per person.*

Ziplining

Zipline Haleakala Tour. For those looking for a different perspective on Haleakala, Skyline Eco-Adventures blends a short hike through a eucalyptus forest with four zipline crossings. During the zipline crossing, you'll be outfitted with a seat harness and connected to a cable, then launched from a 70-foot-high (21m) platform to "zip" along the cable suspended over the slopes of Haleakala. From this viewpoint, you fly over treetops, valleys, gulches, and waterfalls at 10 to 35 mph (16–56kph). These bird's-eye tours operate daily and take riders ages 12 and up, weighing between 80 and 300 pounds. *P.O. Box 880518, Pukalani, HI 96788.* ☎ *808/878-8400. www.skylinehawaii.com. Tour $89 ($80 if you book online).Take Hwy. 37 to Hwy. 377. Turn left on Hwy. 378 for 2.5 miles (4km).*

Ziplining.

Maui's Best **Snorkeling**

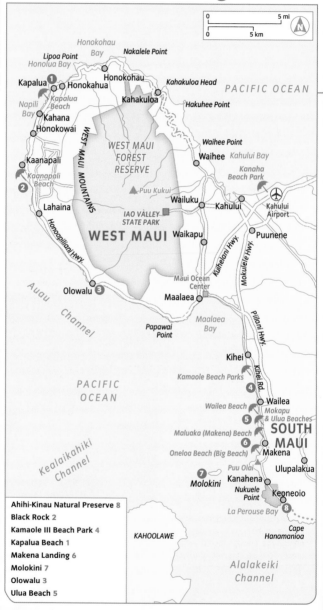

| 0 | | 5 mi |
| 0 | | 5 km |

Honokohau Bay

Lipoa Point
Honolua Bay

Nakalele Point

Kapalua ① Honokahua
Honokohau

Kahakuloa Head

Napili Bay
Kapalua Beach

Kahakuloa

PACIFIC OCEAN

Hakuhee Point

Kahana
Honokowai

WEST MAUI FOREST RESERVE

Waihee Point

Kaanapali

Kaanapali Beach ②

Puu Kukui

Waihee *Kahului Bay*

Kanaha Beach Park

WEST MAUI MOUNTAINS

Wailuku   Kahului

Lahaina

IAO VALLEY STATE PARK

WEST MAUI

Kahului Airport

Honoapiilani Hwy.

Waikapu

Puunene

Maui Ocean Center

Olowalu ③

Maalaea

Kuihelani Hwy.

Mokulele Hwy.

Auau Channel

Papawai Point

Maalaea Bay

Piilani Hwy.

Kihei

PACIFIC OCEAN

Kamaole Beach Parks

Kihei Rd.

④

Wailea

Wailea Beach

Mokapu & Ulua Beaches

⑤

Kealaikahiki Channel

Maluaka (Makena) Beach

SOUTH MAUI

⑥

Oneloa Beach (Big Beach)

Makena

Puu Olai

Ulupalakua

⑦
Molokini

Kanahena

Nukuele Point

Keoneoio

Ahihi-Kinau Natural Preserve 8
Black Rock 2
Kamaole III Beach Park 4
Kapalua Beach 1
Makena Landing 6
Molokini 7
Olowalu 3
Ulua Beach 5

La Perouse Bay

⑧

Cape Hanamanioa

KAHOOLAWE

Alalakeiki Channel

Snorkeling is the main attraction in Maui—and almost anyone can do it. All you need are a mask, a snorkel, fins, and some basic swimming skills. Floating over underwater worlds through colorful clouds of tropical fish is like a dream. If you've never snorkeled before, most resorts and excursion boats offer instruction, but it's plenty easy to figure it out for yourself: In many places all you have to do is wade into the water and look down. Below are my favorite snorkeling spots in Maui.

★ `Ahihi-Kina`u Natural Area Reserve. Ahihi Bay is a 2,000-acre (809ha) state natural area reserve in the lee of Cape Kinau, on Maui's rugged south coast, where Haleakala's red-hot lava ran to the sea in 1790. Fishing is strictly *kapu* (forbidden) here, and the fish know it; they're everywhere in this series of rocky coves and black-lava tide pools. The black, barren, lunarlike land stands in stark contrast to the green-blue water. After you snorkel, check out La Pérouse Bay on the south side of Cape Kinau, where French admiral La Pérouse became the first European to set foot on Maui. As we went to press, the Hawaii State Department of Land and Natural Resources had temporarily restricted access to portions of the reserve until July 31, 2010. For more information call ☎ 808/984-8800 or e-mail ahihikinauinfo@hawaii.gov to get the downloadable brochure on the closure. *Drive south on Makena on Makena Alanui Rd.*

★★ Black Rock. In the Kaanapali Beach Resort, in front of the Sheraton Hotel, Black Rock not only has clear, calm water, but it's also populated with clouds of tropical fish. You might even spot a turtle or two. The third plus for this area is that all the hotels and condominiums lining the ocean here have swimming pools, which means fewer swimmers in the water. *Look for* PUBLIC BEACH ACCESS *signs off Kaanapali*

Pkwy. (off Honoapiilani Hwy./ Hwy.30), in the Kaanapali Resort.

kids Kamaole III Beach Park. You can see why local residents love this beach: Not only does it have wide pockets of golden sand, but it's also the only one with a playground for children and a grassy lawn. For snorkeling, look toward the rocky fingers extending out in the north and south shores; they are fish magnets. *S. Kihei Rd., across from Keonekai Rd., Kihei.*

★★★ Kapalua Beach. I love everything about this beach, located next to the Kapalua Resort. The water is so clear that you can not only see where the gold sands turn to green and then deep blue, but you can also stand on the beach and spot colorful tropical fish. Lava-rock promontories protect the water from strong winds and currents, making it calm for snorkeling, and jutting points at either end of the

Snorkeling in Kihei.

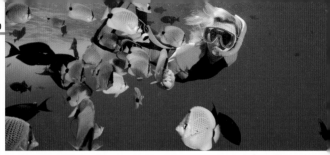

Snorkeling with butterflyfish.

beach attract lots of fish. *Off Lower Honoapiilani Rd., next door to the Napili Kai Beach Resort.*

Makena Landing. This bay is popular with local residents on weekends, but go on a weekday and you could have it all to yourself. My favorite snorkel tour is to follow the rocky shoreline looking for fish. *Along Makena Alanui, look for the shoreline access sign near the Makena Prince Hotel, turn right, and head down to the shore on Makena Rd.*

★★★ **Molokini.** Like a crescent moon fallen from the sky, the crater of Molokini sits almost midway between Maui and the uninhabited island of Kahoolawe. On its concave side Molokini serves as a natural sanctuary for tropical fish and snorkelers, who arrive daily in a fleet of dive boats to this marine-life preserve. Note that in high season, Molokini can be crowded. See the box, "Sail-Snorkel Trips," above for information on getting to Molokini.

Olowalu. Great snorkeling around MM 14, where a turtle-cleaning station is about 150 to 225 feet (46–69m) out from shore. Turtles line up

Where to Get Snorkel Gear

Snorkel Bob's (www.snorkelbob.com) has snorkel gear, boogie boards, and other ocean toys at four locations: Dickenson and Wainee streets, Lahaina (☎ 808/662-0104); Napili Village (5425-C Lower Honoapiilani Hwy., Napili; ☎ 808/669-9603); North Kihei at Azeka Place II (1279 S. Kihei Rd., #310; ☎ 808/875-6188); and South Kihei/Wailea at Kamaole Beach Center (2411 S. Kihei Rd.; ☎ 808/879-7449). All locations are open daily from 8am to 5pm. If you're island hopping, you can rent from a Snorkel Bob's location on one island and return the equipment to a location on another.

If you can't find a Snorkel Bob's close to you, my second pick is **Boss Frog's Dive and Surf Shops** (www.maui-vacation.net), with six stores: Napili (5059 Napilihau St.; ☎ 808/669-4949); Kahana in Kahana Manor Shops (4310 Lower Honoapiilani Rd.; ☎ 808/669-6700); Kaanapali (3636 Lower Honoapiilani Rd.; ☎ 808/665-1200); Lahaina (150 Lahainaluna Rd.; ☎ 808/661-3333); North Kihei in the Longs Drugs Shopping Center (1215 Kihei Rd.; ☎ 808/891-0077); and South Kihei in Dolphin Plaza (2395 S. Kihei Rd., behind Pizza Hut; ☎ 808/875-4477).

Sail-Snorkel Trips

Trilogy ★★★ (☎ 888/MAUI-800 [628-4800] or 808/TRILOGY [874-5649]; www.sailtrilogy.com) tops the list of my favorite snorkel-sail trips. Hop aboard one of the fleet of custom-built catamarans for a half-day trip to Molokini. Trips leave from Maalaea Harbor and include breakfast and a barbecue lunch, and cost $203 for adults and half-price for kids ages 3 to 12.

  Maui Classic Charters ★★ (Maalaea Harbor, slip 55 and slip 80; ☎ 800/736-5740 or 808/879-8188; www.mauicharters.com) offers morning and afternoon snorkel-sail cruises to Molokini on a 55-foot, glass-bottom catamaran. The cost is $89 for adults ($59 for children ages 3–12) for the morning sail and $42 ($30 children) in the afternoon. Trips on the *Four Winds*, a 55-foot glassbottom catamaran, include a continental breakfast; a barbecue lunch; complimentary beer, wine, and soda; complimentary snorkeling gear and instruction; and sport-fishing along the way. Those looking for speed should book a trip on the fast, state-of-the-art catamaran, *Maui Magic.* Maui Classic Charters offers a 5-hour snorkel journey to both Molokini and La Pérouse for $99 for adults and $79 for children ages 5 to 12, including a continental breakfast; barbecue lunch; beer, wine, and soda; snorkel gear; and instruction. During whale season (Dec 22–Apr 22), the *Four Winds* has a 3½-hour whale-watching trip for $42 for adults and $30 for children ages 3 to 12.

  The **Pacific Whale Foundation** (101 N. Kihei Rd., Kihei; ☎ 800/942-5311 or 808/879-8811; www.pacificwhale.org; snorkeling cruises from $80 for all ages) supports its whale research by offering whale-watching cruises and snorkel tours, some to Molokini, on either their 65-foot power catamaran, or a 50-foot sailing catamaran, or another boat from their fleet. Choose from 15 daily trips, offered December through May, out of both Lahaina and Maalaea harbors.

  For a high-speed, action-packed snorkel-sail experience, consider the **Pride of Maui** (Maalaea Harbor; ☎ 877/TO-PRIDE [867-7433] or 808/875-0955; www.prideofmaui.com), a 65-foot power boat. It offers 5½-hour snorkel cruises that take in not only Molokini, but also Turtle Bay and Makena. The cost is $90 for ages 13 and up ($80 if you book on the website) and $56 for ages 3 to 12. Continental breakfast, barbecue lunch, gear, and instruction are included. There is also an afternoon Molokini cruise ($35 for ages 13 and up; $27 for ages 3–12, plus an optional lunch for an additional $5).

here to have cleaner wrasses pick off small parasites. *MM 14, Honoapiilani Hwy. 5 miles (8km) south of Lahaina.*

Ulua Beach. Snorkel here in the morning when the waters are calm and before local winds kick up around noon. *Look for the blue shoreline access sign, on Wailea Alanui Dr., Wailea.*

Adventures in the Ocean

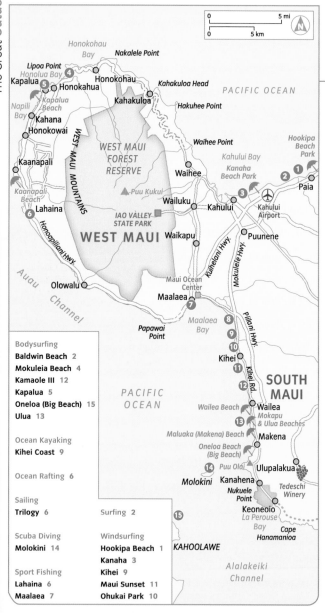

```
0          5 mi
0          5 km
```

Honokohau Bay
Nakalele Point
Lipoa Point
Honolua Bay 4
Kapalua 5 Honokahua
Honokohau
Kahakuloa Head
Napili Bay
Kapalua Beach
Kahakuloa
Hakuhee Point
Kahana
Honokowai
Waihee Point
Kahului Bay
Hookipa Beach Park
WEST MAUI FOREST RESERVE
Kaanapali
Kanaha Beach Park
2 1
Kaanapali Beach
WEST MAUI MOUNTAINS
Puu Kukui
Waihee
3
Paia
Lahaina 6
Wailuku Kahului
Kahului Airport
IAO VALLEY STATE PARK
Honoapiilani Hwy.
WEST MAUI
Waikapu
Puunene
Kaului Hwy.
Mokulele Hwy.
Auau Channel
Olowalu
Maui Ocean Center
Maalaea 7
Papawai Point
Maalaea Bay
8
9
Piilani Hwy.
Bodysurfing
Baldwin Beach 2
Mokuleia Beach 4
Kamaole III 12
Kapalua 5
Oneloa (Big Beach) 15
Ulua 13
Kihei
10
11
Kihei Rd.
12
SOUTH MAUI
PACIFIC OCEAN
Wailea Beach
Wailea
Mokapu & Ulua Beaches
Maluaka (Makena) Beach
Makena
Ocean Kayaking
Kihei Coast 9

Ocean Rafting 6

Sailing
Trilogy 6

Scuba Diving
Molokini 14

Sport Fishing
Lahaina 6
Maalaea 7
13
Oneloa Beach (Big Beach)
14
Puu Olai
Molokini
Ulupalakua
Kanahena
Tedeschi Winery
Nukele Point
Keoneoio
La Perouse Bay
Cape Hanamanioa
15
KAHOOLAWE
Alalakeiki Channel

Surfing 2

Windsurfing
Hookipa Beach 1
Kanaha 3
Kihei 9
Maui Sunset 11
Ohukai Park 10

PACIFIC OCEAN

To really appreciate Maui, you need to get off the land and into the sea. Trade winds off the Lahaina coast and the strong wind that rips through Maui's isthmus make sailing around the island exciting. Or you can go head-to-head with a 1,000-pound marlin in a big game fishing battle; slowly glide over the water in a kayak; hover high above it in a parasail; or get into the water and scuba dive, bodysurf, board surf, or windsurf.

Bodysurfing. Riding the waves without a board, becoming one with the rolling water is a way of life in Hawaii. Some bodysurfers just rely on their hands to ride the waves; others use hand boards or a boogie board or body board. Both bodysurfing and body boarding require a pair of open-heeled swim fins to help propel you through the water. The best bodysurfing beaches are **Baldwin Beach,** just outside of Paia, which has great waves nearly year-round; and in winter, **Mokuleia Beach,** known locally as Slaughterhouse (for the cattle slaughterhouse that once stood here, not because of the waves—although they are definitely for expert bodysurfers only). Storms from the south bring fair bodysurfing conditions and great boogie boarding to the lee side of Maui: **Oneloa (Big Beach)** in Makena, **Ulua** and **Kamaole III** in Kihei, and **Kapalua** beaches are all good choices.

Ocean Kayaking. Gliding silently over the water, propelled by a paddle, seeing Maui from the sea the way the early Hawaiians did— that's what ocean kayaking is all about. One of Maui's best kayak routes is along the **Kihei Coast,** where there's easy access to calm water. Go out in the early mornings; the wind comes up around 11am, making seas choppy and paddling difficult.

Ocean Rafting. If you're semi-adventurous and looking for a more intimate experience with the sea, try ocean rafting. The inflatable rafts hold 6 to 24 passengers. Tours usually include snorkeling and coastal cruising. One of the best (and most reasonable) outfitters is **Hawaiian Ocean Raft;** its 5-hour tour includes three stops for snorkeling and stops to search for dolphins, plus continental breakfast and midmorning snacks. *Lahaina Harbor.* ☎ *888/677-RAFT (7238) or 808/667-2191. www.hawaii oceanrafting.com. From $74 for adults, from $53 for children 5–12.*

Craft along the Kihei Coast.

Kayak Tours

My favorite kayak tour operator is Makena Kayak Tours (☎ 877/879-8426 or 808/879-8426; www.makenakayaks.com). Professional guide Dino Ventura leads a 2½-hour trip from Makena Landing and loves taking first-timers over the secluded coral reefs and into remote coves. His wonderful tour will be a highlight of your vacation. The tour costs $85 for all ages, including refreshments and snorkel and kayak equipment. In Hana, **Hana-Maui Kayak & Snorkel Adventures** (☎ 808/248-7711; www.hanaseasport.com) runs 2-hour tours of Hana's coastline on wide, stable "no-roll" kayaks, with snorkeling. The cost is $108 per person all ages (all equipment included).

Parasailing. Soar high above the crowds (at around 400 ft./122m) for a bird's-eye view of Maui. This ocean adventure sport, which is something of a cross between skydiving and water-skiing, involves sailing through the air, suspended under a large parachute attached by a towline to a speedboat. Keep in mind, though, that parasailing tours don't run during whale season, which is roughly December through May. Book my favorite, the early-bird special (when the light is fantastic and the price is right) at 8am with **UFO Parasail**, which picks you up at Kaanapali Beach. ☎ *800/FLY-4-UFO (359-4836) or 808/661-7-UFO (661-7836). www. ufoparasail.net. Early-bird special $65 for 400 ft. (122m) or $75 for 800 ft. (244m).*

Sailing. Trilogy ★★★ offers my favorite snorkel-sail trips. See the box on p 101 for more information.

Scuba Diving. You can see a great variety of tropical marine life—more than 100 endemic species found

A playful whale.

nowhere else on the planet—explore sea caves, and swim with sea turtles and monk seals in the clear tropical waters off the island. Trade winds often rough up the seas in the afternoon, so most operators schedule early-morning dives that end at noon. **Molokini** (p 100), a marine-life park, is one of Hawaii's top dive spots. This crescent-shaped crater has three tiers of diving: a 35-foot (11m) plateau inside the crater basin (used by beginning divers and snorkelers), a wall sloping to 70 feet (21m) just beyond the inside plateau, and a sheer wall on the outside and backside of the crater that plunges 350 feet (107m). This underwater park is very popular thanks to calm, clear, protected waters and an abundance of marine life, from manta rays to clouds of yellow butterflyfish. Most operators offer no-experience-necessary dives, ranging from $100 for one tank to $150 for two tanks. Maui's two best scuba operators are **Ed Robinson's Diving Adventures**

You might encounter a white tip reef shark like this one while diving.

(☎ 800/635-1273; www.mauiscuba.com), charging $130 for two-tank dives ($135 with equipment); and **Mike Severns Diving** (☎ 808/879-6596; www.mikeseversnsdiving.com), where two-tank dives are

Whale-Watching

Every winter, pods of Pacific humpback whales make the 3,000-mile (4,828km) swim from the chilly waters of Alaska to bask in Maui's summery shallows. The whale-watching season usually begins in December or January and lasts until April or May. Bring binoculars to one of the following spots: **McGregor Point,** on the way to Lahaina, scenic lookout at MM 9; **Olowalu Reef,** along the straight part of Honoapiilani Highway, between McGregor Point and Olowalu; **Puu Olai ★★,** which is a tough climb, but the island's best spot for offshore whale-watching; or **Wailea Marriott Resort** (3700 Wailea Alanui Dr., Wailea), on the Wailea coastal walk, with a telescope installed for whale-watching.

If you want to get a closer look, try the cruises offered by the nonprofit **Pacific Whale Foundation** (101 N. Kihei Rd., Kihei; ☎ 800/942-5311 or 808/879-8811; www.pacificwhale.org). The rate is $80 for all ages. Cruises are offered from December through May, out of both Lahaina and Maalaea harbors.

$130 with your own equipment and $145 with rental equipment.

Sportfishing. Marlin (as big as 1,200 lb.), tuna, *ono,* and mahimahi swim in Maui's coastal and channel waters. No license is required; just book a sportfishing vessel out of **Lahaina** or **Maalaea** harbors. Most charter boats that troll for big-game fish carry a maximum of six passengers. You can walk the docks, inspecting boats and talking to captains and crews, or book through **Sportfish Hawaii** (☎ 877/388-1376 or 808/396-2607; www.sport fishhawaii.com). Prices vary widely according to the boat, the crowd, and the captain. A shared boat for a half-day of fishing starts at $139. A half-day exclusive (you get the entire boat) starts at $850; a full-day exclusive starts at $999. Many boat captains tag and release marlin or keep the fish for themselves (sorry, that's Hawaii style). If you want to eat your mahimahi for dinner or have your marlin mounted, tell the captain before you go.

Surfing. The ancient Hawaiian sport of *hee nalu* (wave sliding) is probably the sport most people picture when they think of the islands. If you'd like to give it a shot, call Tide and Kiva Rivers, two local boys (actually twins), who have been surfing since they could walk, and the best surf instructors I have seen. The lessons are 2 hours long and include equipment and instruction. Tide says they decide where the lesson will take place based on their client's ability and where the surf is on that day. He says he has beginners standing up in their first lesson. *Rivers to the Sea.* ☎ *808/280-8795 or 808/280-6236. www.riverstothe sea.com. 2-hr. private instruction $160, 2-hr. lesson for a couple $220.*

Windsurfing. Maui has Hawaii's best windsurfing beaches. In winter,

windsurfers from around the world flock to the town of Paia to ride the waves. Hookipa Beach, known all over the globe for its brisk winds and excellent waves, is the site of several world-championship contests. Kanaha, west of Kahului Airport, also has dependable winds. When the winds turn northerly, Kihei is the spot to be. The northern end of Kihei is best: Ohukai Park, the first beach as you enter South Kihei Road from the northern end, has not only good winds but also parking, a long strip of grass to assemble your gear, and good access to the water. Experienced windsurfers can be found in front of the Maui Sunset condo (1032 S. Kihei Rd., near Waipuilani St. and a block north of McDonald's), which has great windsurfing conditions but a very shallow reef (not good for beginners). For lessons contact Hawaiian Island Surf and Sport, *415 Dairy Rd., Kahului.* ☎ *800/231-6958 or 808/871-4981. www.hawaiianisland.com. 2½-hr. lesson $89, $89 and up for longer or private lesson.* ●

Watching windsurfers is almost as much fun as trying the sport yourself.

7 The Best **Lodging**

Lodging Best Bets

Most Romantic
★ Hamoa Bay Bungalow $$ *Hana Highway, Hana (p 112)*

Most Historic
★★ Old Wailuku Inn at Ulupono $$ *2199 Kahookele St., Wailuku (p 115)*

Most Luxurious Hotel
★★★ The Fairmont Kea Lani Maui $$$$ *4100 Wailea Alanui Dr., Wailea (p 112)*

Most Luxurious Condo
★★ Kaanapali Alii $$$$ *50 Nohea Kai Dr., Kaanapali (p 114)*

Best Moderate Hotel
★ Lahaina Inn $$ *127 Lahainaluna Rd., Lahaina (p 114)*

Best Budget Hotel
★ Nona Lani Cottages $ *455 S. Kihei Rd., Kihei (p 115)*

Best for Kids
★★★ Four Seasons Resort Maui at Wailea $$$$ *3900 Wailea Alanui Dr., Wailea (p 112)*

Best Value
★★ Pineapple Inn Maui $ *3170 Akala Dr., Kihei (p 115)*

Most Charming B&B
★★ Wild Ginger Falls $ *355 Kaluanui Rd., Makawao (p 116)*

Best View
★★ Napili Kai Beach Resort $$$ *5900 Honoapiilani Rd., Napili (p 115)*

Best Club-Level Amenities
★★★ Ritz-Carlton Kapalua $$$$ *1 Ritz-Carlton Dr., Kapalua (p 116)*

Best Service
★★★ Four Seasons Resort Maui at Wailea $$$$ *3900 Wailea Alanui Dr., Wailea (p 112)*

Best Spa
★★★ Grand Wailea Resort Hotel & Spa $$$$ *3850 Wailea Alanui Dr., Wailea (p 112)*

Most Hawaiian Resort
★★★ Hotel Hana-Maui $$$$ *Hana Hwy., Hana (p 113);* and ★ Kaanapali Beach Hotel $$ *2525 Kaanapali Pkwy., Kaanapali (p 114)*

Best Fantasy Resort
★★ Hyatt Regency Maui Resort and Spa $$$$ *200 Nohea Kai Dr., Kaanapali (p 113)*

Best Off the Beaten Path
★★ The Inn at Mama's Fish House $$ *799 Poho Place, Kuau (p 113)*

Most Ecofriendly
★ Westin Maui $$$$ *2365 Kaanapali Pkwy., Kaanapali (p 116)*

Most Serene Location
★★ Hana Oceanfront $$ *Haneoo Rd., Hana (p 113)*

Best Family Condo
★ Maui Eldorado Resort $$$ *2661 Kekaa Dr., Kaanapali (p 114)*

The Kaanapali Beach Hotel.

Maui & Kapalua Lodging

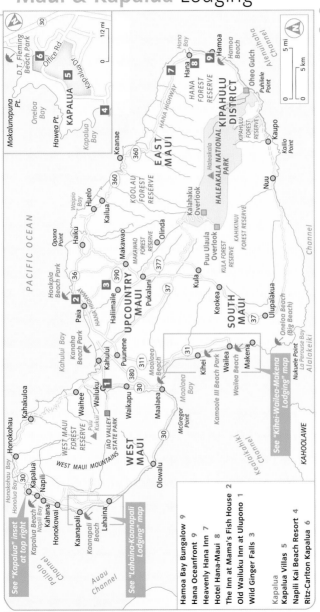

Hamoa Bay Bungalow 9
Hana Oceanfront 9
Heavenly Hana Inn 7
Hotel Hana-Maui 8
The Inn at Mama's Fish House 2
Old Wailuku Inn at Ulupono 1
Wild Ginger Falls 3

Kapalua
Kapalua Villas 5
Napili Kai Beach Resort 4
Ritz-Carlton Kapalua 6

Photo p 107: The Fairmont Kea Lani Maui.

Lahaina & Kaanapali Lodging

Best Western Pioneer Inn 10
Hyatt Regency Maui Resort and Spa 7
Kaanapali Alii 6
Kaanapali Beach Hotel 3
Lahaina Inn 8
Maui Eldorado Resort 1
The Plantation Inn 9
Sheraton Maui 2
Westin Maui 5
The Whaler on Kaanapali Beach 4

Kihei/Wailea/Makena Lodging

The Fairmont Kea Lani Maui 6
Four Seasons Resort Maui at Wailea 5
Grand Wailea Resort Hotel & Spa 4
Maui Prince Hotel 7
Nona Lani Cottages 1
Pineapple Inn Maui 2
Wailea Marriott Resort & Spa 3

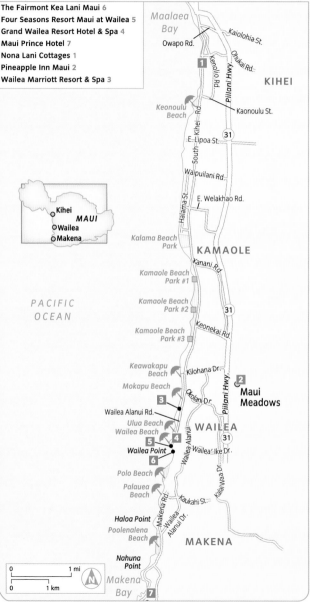

Maui Hotels A to Z

kids Best Western Pioneer Inn LAHAINA   This turn-of-the-19th-century, two-story, plantation-style hotel overlooking Lahaina Harbor has been remodeled with vintage bathrooms. *658 Wharf St. (in front of Lahaina Pier).* ☎ *800/457-5457 or 808/661-3636. www.pioneerinnmaui. com. 34 units. Doubles $145–$205. Extra person $15 (ages 12 and over). AE, DC, DISC, MC, V. Map p 110.*

★★★ The Fairmont Kea Lani Maui WAILEA   You get your money's worth at this luxurious resort: an entire suite—plus a kitchenette, entertainment center, sofa bed, spacious bedroom, and large lanai. *4100 Wailea Alanui Dr.* ☎ *800/659-4100 or 808/875-4100. www.fairmont. com/kealani. 450 units. Doubles $485–$1,100. AE, DC, DISC, MC, V. Map p 111.*

★★★ kids Four Seasons Resort Maui at Wailea WAILEA   The Four Seasons has attentive but not cloying service, and it's the most kid-friendly hotel on Maui, with cookies and milk on arrival, children's menus, and complimentary baby gear (cribs to strollers). You can even prepurchase necessities like diapers and baby food; the hotel will have them waiting for you when you arrive. *3900 Wailea Alanui Dr.* ☎ *800/334-MAUI (6284) or 808/874-8000. www.fourseasons.com/maui. 380 units. Doubles $495–$970. AE, DC, MC, V. Map p 111.*

★★★ Grand Wailea Resort Hotel & Spa WAILEA   Hawaii's largest and most elaborate spa, with every kind of body treatment you can imagine, plus the use of the numerous baths, hot tubs, mineral pools, saunas, and steam rooms. *3850 Wailea Alanui Dr.* ☎ *800/888-6100 or 808/875-1234. www.grand wailea.com. 780 units. Doubles $459–$1,080. AE, DC, DISC, MC, V. Map p 111.*

★ Hamoa Bay House & Bungalow HANA   Romance blooms in a 600-square-foot (56-sq.-m) Balinese-style treetop studio with a hot tub

Porch deck at the Four Seasons Resort.

A room at the Hotel Hana-Maui.

and a beckoning bamboo bed. Plus, you're close to Hamoa Beach. *P.O. Box 773.* ☎ *808/248-7853. www. hamoabay.com. 2 units. Doubles $225–$285. MC, V. Map p 109.*

★★ **Hana Oceanfront** HANA Serenity reigns at these two comfy, plantation-style cottages (with polished bamboo flooring and fully appointed gourmet kitchens), just across the street from Hamoa Bay. *P.O. Box 843.* ☎ *808/248-7558. www. myoceancottage.com. 2 units. Doubles $250–$275. MC, V. Map p 109.*

★★ **Heavenly Hana Inn** HANA In this Japanese-style inn each suite has a sitting room, polished hardwood floors, a separate bedroom with a raised platform bed, and a black-marble soaking tub. *P.O. Box 790.* ☎ *808/248-8442. www.heavenly hanainn.com. 3 units. Doubles $190–$260. AE, DISC, MC, V. Map p 109.*

★★★ **kids Hotel Hana-Maui** HANA   The atmosphere and the culture of old Hawaii is set within 21st-century accommodations on 66 rolling seaside acres (27ha).

Throw in an excellent spa, and one of Hana's best beaches, and you'll never want to leave. *P.O. Box 9.* ☎ *800/321-HANA (4262) or 808/248-8211. www.hotelhanamaui.com. 66 units. Doubles $495–$1,675. AE, DC, DISC, MC, V. Map p 109.*

★★ **kids Hyatt Regency Maui Resort & Spa** KAANAPALI   This fantasy resort has a ½-acre (.2ha) outdoor pool with a 150-foot (46m) lava tube slide, a cocktail bar under the falls, nine waterfalls, exotic birds in the lobby, and an eclectic Asian and Pacific art collection. *200 Nohea Kai Dr.* ☎ *800/233-1234 or 808/661-1234. www.maui.hyatt.com. 806 units. Doubles $435–$715. AE, DC, DISC, MC, V. Map p 110.*

★★ **The Inn at Mama's Fish House** PAIA   Off the beaten path in a coconut grove on secluded Kuau Beach, these expertly decorated duplexes sit next door to Mama's Fish House (guests get a discount on meals). *799 Poho Place (off the Hana Hwy. in Kuau).* ☎ *800/860-HULA (4852) or 808/579-9764. www.mamasfishhouse.com. 6 units. Doubles $175–$475. AE, DISC, MC, V. Map p 109.*

The pool at the Grand Wailea Resort.

★★ **kids Kaanapali Alii** KAANA-PALI These oceanfront condominium units sit on 8 landscaped acres (3.2ha) right on Kaanapali Beach and combine all the amenities of a luxury hotel with the convenience of a condominium. There's even a yoga class on the oceanfront lawn. *50 Nohea Kai Dr.* ☎ *800/642-6284 or 808/661-3330. www.kaanapali-alii. com. 264 units. $1,185–$1,845 1 bedroom for 4; $1,329–$2,835 2 bedroom for 6. AE, DC, DISC, MC, V. Map p 110.*

★ **kids Kaanapali Beach Hotel** KAANAPALI Old Hawaii values and customs reign here; you'll see them in everything from the nightly Hawaiian hula and music to the extensive Hawaiiana program (learn to cut pineapple, weave *lauhala,* even dance the *real* hula). *2525 Kaanapali Pkwy.* ☎ *800/262-8450 or 808/661-0011. www.kbhmaui.com. 430 units. Doubles $225–$355. AE, DC, DISC, MC, V. Map p 110.*

★★ **kids Kapalua Villas** KAPALUA The palatial condo units dotting the oceanfront cliffs and fairways of this idyllic coast are a (relative) bargain, especially for big families. *500 Office Rd.* ☎ *800/545-0018 or 808/669-8088. www.kapaluavillas.com. $279–$559 1-bedroom; $389–$759 2-bedroom; $549–$799 3-bedroom. AE, DC, DISC, MC, V. Map p 109.*

★ **Lahaina Inn** LAHAINA These Victorian antique–stuffed rooms are a rare bargain on Maui, with an excellent restaurant and bar downstairs (Lahaina Grill, p 125). However, rooms are on the small side. *127 Lahainaluna Rd. (near Front St.).* ☎ *800/669-3444 or 808/661-0577. www.lahainainn.com. 12 units. Doubles $150–$170. AE, MC, V. Map p 110.*

★ **kids Maui Outrigger Eldorado Resort** KAANAPALI These are the best condos for families: spacious units, grassy play areas outside, safe swimming, and a beachfront with cabanas and barbecue area. *2661 Kekaa Dr.* ☎ *800/688-7444 or 808/661-0021. www.outrigger.com. 204 units.*

Kapalua Villas.

Napili Kai Beach Resort.

$169–$309 studio; $199–$379 1 bedroom (up to 4); $379–$509 2 bedroom (up to 6). $219. AE, DC, DISC, MC, V. Map p 110.

★★ **Maui Prince Hotel** MAKENA Tranquillity and a golden-sand beach are what you'll find at this end-of-the-road resort where every clutter-free room has an ocean view. *5400 Makena Alanui.* ☎ 800/321-6284 or 808/874-1111. www.mauiprince hotel.com. 310 units. Doubles $425–$600. AE, DC, MC, V. Map p 111.

★★ kids **Napili Kai Beach Resort** NAPILI Ocean views of Molokai and Lanai, Hawaii-style architecture, a secluded gold-sand beach, and a choice of hotel rooms or condos make this resort very popular. *5900 Honoapiilani Rd. (at the extreme north end of Napili, next to Kapalua Resort).* ☎ 800/367-5030 or 808/669-6271. www.napilikai. com. 162 units. $230–$335 double; $325–$430 studio (sleeps 3–4); $455–$650 1-bedroom suite (sleeps up to 5); $655–$965 2-bedroom suite (sleeps up to 7). AE, DISC, MC, V. Map p 109.

★ **Nona Lani Cottages** KIHEI These self-contained cottages tucked among palm, fruit, and sweet-smelling flower trees and across the street from a white-sand beach, are the best deal on Maui. *455 S. Kihei Rd. (just south of Hwy. 31), P.O. Box 655.* ☎ 800/733-2688 or 808/879-2497. www.nonalani cottages.com. 11 units. Double $120–$150. No credit cards. Map p 111.

★★ **Old Wailuku Inn at Ulupono** WAILUKU   This lovingly restored 1924 former plantation manager's home offers a genuine old Hawaii experience, plus a gourmet breakfast. *2199 Kahookele St. (at High St., across from the Wailuku School).* ☎ 800/305-4899 or 808/244-5897. www.mauiinn.com. 10 units. Doubles $150–$190. MC, V. Map p 109.

★★ **Pineapple Inn Maui** KIHEI This charming inn offers impeccably decorated, soundproof rooms, a giant saltwater pool and Jacuzzi overlooking the ocean, and wallet-pleasing prices. *3170 Akala Dr.* ☎ 877/212-MAUI (6284) or 808/298-4403. www.pineappleinnmaui.com. Doubles $139–$149; cottage $215. No credit cards. Map p 111.

★★ **The Plantation Inn** LAHAINA This romantic, Victorian-style inn features period furniture and four-poster canopy beds. It's next door to one of Lahaina's best French restaurants, Gerard's (p 124), where guests get a discount. *174 Lahainaluna Rd. (btw. Wainee and Luakini sts., 1 block from Hwy. 30).* ☎ 800/433-6815 or 808/667-9225. www.the plantationinn.com. 19 units. Doubles $169–$255. AE, DC, DISC, MC, V. Map p 110.

★★★ kids Ritz-Carlton Kapalua

KAPALUA   If you can afford it, stay on the Club Floor, which offers the best amenities in the state, including French-roast coffee in the morning, a buffet at lunch, cookies in the afternoon, and pupus and drinks at sunset. *1 Ritz-Carlton Dr.* ☎ *800/262-8440 or 808/669-6200. www.ritzcarlton.com. 548 units. Doubles $350–$705; Club Floor $695–$895. AE, DC, DISC, MC, V. Map p 109.*

★★ kids Sheraton Maui

KAANAPALI   The family suites are great for those traveling with kids: three beds, a sitting room with full-size couch, and two TVs (both equipped with Nintendo); plus fun activities ranging from Hawaiian games to visits to nearby attractions. *2605 Kaanapali Pkwy.* ☎ *888/488-3535 or 808/661-0031. www.sheraton-maui.com. 510 units. Doubles $234–$540. AE, DC, DISC, MC, V. Map p 110.*

★★ Wailea Beach Marriott Resort & Spa

WAILEA   This classic open-air, 1970s-style hotel in a tropical garden by the sea gives you a sense of what Maui was like before the big resort boom. *3700 Wailea Alanui Dr.* ☎ *800/367-2960 or 808/879-1922. www.marriotthawaii.com. 545 units. Doubles $385–$735. AE, DC, DISC, MC, V. Map p 111.*

★ kids Westin Maui

KAANAPALI   This resort emphasizes a healthy environment, and smoking is no longer allowed in guest rooms (it is allowed in some public areas). Kids will love the aquatic playground. *2365 Kaanapali Pkwy.* ☎ *888/625-4949 or 808/667-2525. www.westinmaui.com. 758 units. Doubles $240–$920. AE, DC, DISC, MC, V. Map p 110.*

★★ The Whaler on Kaanapali Beach

KAANAPALI   In the heart of Kaanapali, right on the world-famous beach, lies this condo oasis of elegance, privacy, and luxury. *2481 Kaanapali Pkwy. (next to Whalers Village).* ☎ *877/997-6667 or 808/661-4861. www.resortquesthawaii.com. 360 units. $176–$224 studio; $198–$283 1 bedroom (up to 4); $260–$429 2 bedroom (up to 6). AE, DC, DISC, MC, V. Map p 110.*

★★ Wild Ginger Falls

MAKAWAO   Perfect for honeymooners and lovers, this cozy, romantic, intimate cottage, hidden in Miliko Gulch, overlooks a stream with a waterfall, bamboo, sweet-smelling ginger, and banana trees. *355 Kaluanui Rd.* ☎ *808/573-1173. www.wildgingerfalls.com. 1 unit. Double $145–$155. No credit cards. Map p 109.* ●

A room at the Ritz-Carlton Kapalua.

Dining Best Bets

Best on the Beach
★ Hula Grill $$$ *Whalers Village, Kaanapali (p 124)*

Best Breakfast
★ Charlie's Restaurant $$ *142 Hana Hwy., Paia (p 123)*; and ★★ Longhi's $$$$ *Shops at Wailea (p 126)*

Best Burger
Cheeseburger in Paradise $ *811 Front St., Lahaina (p 123)*

Best Budget Deli
★ CJ's Deli and Diner $ *Kaanapali Fairway Shops (p 123)*

Best Crepes
★★ Café des Amis $$ *42 Baldwin, Paia (p 123)*

Best for Families
★ Stella Blues $$ *Azeka II Shopping Center, Kihei (p 128)*

Best French
★★★ Gerard's $$$$ *174 Lahain-aluna Rd., Lahaina (p 124)*

Freshest Fish
★★★ Pineapple Grill Kapalua $$$ *200 Kapalua Dr. (p 127)*

Best Luau
★★★ Old Lahaina Luau $$$$ *1251 Front St., Lahaina (p 124)*

Best Fast Mexican
Maui Tacos $ *Napili Lahaina Kihei Kahului (p 126)*

Best People-Watching
★ Milagros Food Company $$ *Hana Highway, Paia (p 127)*

Best Pizza
Shaka Sandwich & Pizza $$ *1770 S. Kihei Rd., Kihei (p 128)*

Most Romantic
★★ Mala Wailea $$$ *Wailea Beach Marriott, Wailea (p 126)*

Best Splurge
★★★ Mama's Fish House $$$$ *799 Poho Place, Kuau (p 126)*

Best Sushi
★★ Sansei Seafood Restaurant and Sushi Bar $$$ *Office Road, Kapalua (p 128)*

Most Trendy
★★ David Paul's Island Grill $$$ *Lahaina Center, 900 Front St., Lahaina (p 123)*

Best Meal Under $10
Joy's Place $ *1993 S. Kihei Rd., Kihei (p 125)*

Best View
★★ Kula Lodge $$$ *Haleakala Highway, Kula (p 125)*

Enjoying a sunset meal at the Pineapple Grill.

Maui & Paia Dining

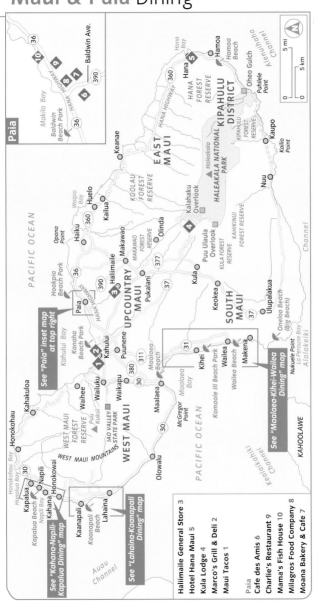

Paia
Cafe des Amis 6
Charlie's Restaurant 9
Mama's Fish House 10
Milagros Food Company 8
Moana Bakery & Cafe 7

Haliimaile General Store 3
Hotel Hana Maui 5
Kula Lodge 4
Marco's Grill & Deli 2
Maui Tacos 1

Photo p 117: Fettuccine at the Lahaina Grill.

The Best Dining

Lahaina & Kaanapali
Dining

CJ's Deli and Diner 1
Cheeseburger in Paradise 9
Chez Paul 13
David Paul's Island Grill 5
The Feast at Lele 12
Gerard's 8
Hula Grill 2
Lahaina Coolers 11
Lahaina Grill 7
Lahaina Store Grille and Oyster Bar 10
Maui Tacos 6
Old Lahaina Luau 4
Umalu 3

Kahana, Napili & Kapalua
Dining

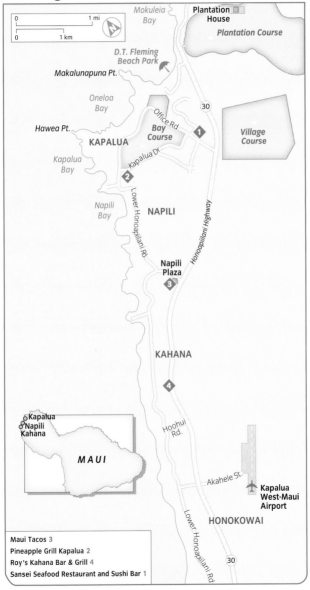

Maui Tacos 3
Pineapple Grill Kapalua 2
Roy's Kahana Bar & Grill 4
Sansei Seafood Restaurant and Sushi Bar 1

Maalaea, Kihei & Wailea
Dining

Joe's Bar & Grill 11
Joy's Place 6
Ko 10
Longhi's 9
Mala Wailea 8
Maui Tacos 7
Peggy Sue's 3
Sansei Seafood & Sushi Bar 5
Stella Blues Cafe 2
Shaka Sandwich & Pizza 4
The Waterfront at Maalaea 1

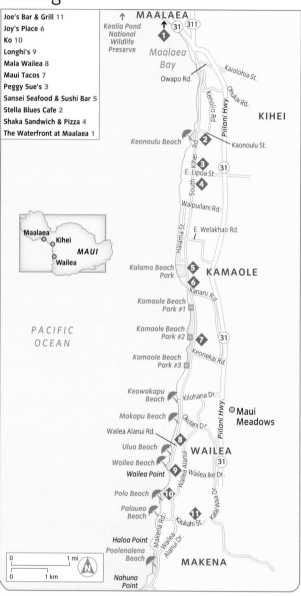

Maui Restaurants A to Z

★ **kids CJ's Deli and Diner**
KAANAPALI *AMERICAN/DELI* It's worth the drive to sample the comfort food at this hip, happening deli, with prices so low you won't believe you're still on Maui. *Kaanapali Fairway Shops, 2580 Keka'a Dr. (just off the Honoapiilani Hwy./Hwy. 30.).* ☎ *808/667-0968. Entrees $5–$10. AE, MC, V. Breakfast, lunch & dinner daily. Map p 120.*

★★ **Cafe des Amis** PAIA *CREPES/ MEDITERRANEAN/INDIAN* Crepes are the stars here, just edging out the incredibly cheap authentic Indian curries. Finish with the best coffee in Paia. *42 Baldwin Ave.* ☎ *808/579-6323. Entrees $10–$17. MC, V. Breakfast, lunch & dinner daily. Map p 119.*

★ **kids Charlie's Restaurant**
PAIA *AMERICAN/MEXICAN* Offering one of the best breakfasts on Maui, this landmark is a mix of a 1960s hippie hangout, a windsurfers' power-breakfast spot, and a honky-tonk bar that gets going after dark. *142 Hana Hwy.* ☎ *808/579-9453. Entrees $5–$20. AE, DISC, MC, V. Breakfast, lunch & dinner daily. Map p 119.*

kids Cheeseburger in Paradise
LAHAINA *AMERICAN* Always crowded and noisy (with live music every night), this shrine to the American classic is a good value. It has great grinds and a killer ocean view. *811 Front St.* ☎ *808/661-4855. Burgers $9–$13. AE, DISC, MC, V. Breakfast, lunch & dinner daily. Map p 120.*

★★ **Chez Paul** OLOWALU *FRENCH* In the middle of nowhere, this classic French restaurant offers elegant food in a casual setting, pricey but worth every penny. *MM 15, Honoapiilani Hwy.* ☎ *808/661-3843. www.chezpaul.net. Entrees $29–$38. DISC, MC, V. Dinner daily. Map p 120.*

★★ **David Paul's Island Grill**
LAHAINA *NEW ISLAND CUISINE* One of Hawaii's top chefs has opened a new restaurant in Lahaina, introducing his "new island cooking," a combination of American cuisine and island products. Chef David has an exhibit kitchen, so you can watch all the action. *Lahaina Center, 900 Front St., Ste. A-101, Lahaina.* ☎ *808/662-3000. www.davidpauls islandgrill.com. Entrees $29–$38. AE, DC, DISC, MC, V. Lunch & dinner daily. Map p 120.*

★★ **The Feast at Lele** LAHAINA *POLYNESIAN* Taking Luau cuisine to a new level, the owners of Old Lahaina Luau (p 124) provide the food and dances from Hawaii, Tonga, Tahiti, Cook, New Zealand, and Samoa in an outdoor setting with white-clothed, candlelit tables set on the sand and entrees from each island. *505 Front St.* ☎ *886/ 244-5353 or 808/667-5353. www. feastatlele.com. Set 5-course menu*

Haliimaile General Store.

Old Lahaina Luau

Maui's best luau features terrific food and entertainment in a peerless, ocean-front setting. The luau begins at sunset and features Tahitian and Hawaiian entertainment, including ancient hula, hula from the missionary era, modern hula, and an intelligent narrative on the dance's rocky course of survival into modern times. The entertainment is riveting, even for jaded locals. The high-quality food, served from an open-air thatched structure, is as much Pacific Rim as authentically Hawaiian: imu-roasted kalua pig, baked mahimahi in Maui-onion cream sauce, guava chicken, teriyaki sirloin steak, lomi salmon, poi, dried fish, *poke,* Hawaiian sweet potato, sautéed vegetables, seafood salad, and the ultimate treat, taro leaves with coconut milk. Old Lahaina Luau (1251 Front St., Lahaina; ☎ 800/248-5828 or 808/667-1998; www.oldlahainaluau.com). costs $96 for adults and $65 for children 12 and under.

The Old Lahaina Luau is a feast for the eyes and the palate.

$115 adults, $80 children 2–12; gratuity not included. AE, MC, V. Dinner daily. Map p 120.

★★★ **Gerard's** LAHAINA *FRENCH* Chef Gerard Reversade (a frequent winner of the *Wine Spectator* Award of Excellence) is at the helm of this creative French cuisine in an elegant Victorian home. *In the Plantation Inn, 174 Lahainaluna Rd.* ☎ *808/661-8939. www.gerardsmaui.com. Entrees $33–$54. AE, DC, DISC, MC, V. Dinner daily. Map p 120.*

★★★ kids **Haliimaile General Store** HALIIMAILE *AMERICAN* Chef Bev Gannon, 1 of the 12 original Hawaii Regional Cuisine chefs, heads up this foodie haven in the pineapple fields with her innovative spin on good ol' American cuisine, bringing Hawaiian and Texas flavors together. *Haliimaile Rd.* ☎ *808/572-2666. www.haliimailegeneralstore. com. Entrees $15–$40. AE, DC, DISC,*

MC, V. Lunch Mon–Fri; dinner daily. Map p 119.

★★★ **Hotel Hana-Maui** HANA *ECLECTIC* This ingredient-driven menu (fresh fish caught by local fishermen, produce grown by nearby farmers, and fruits in season) is served in the graceful setting of the open-aired, large window dining room. Not cheap, but worth it. *Hana Hwy.* ☎ *808/248-8211. Entrees $12–$40. AE, DISC, MC, V. Breakfast, lunch & dinner daily. Friday buffet $50 and Hawaiian show 6–8:30pm. Map p 119.*

★ kids **Hula Grill** KAANAPALI *HAWAII REGIONAL/SEAFOOD* Skip the main dining room and dig your toes in the sand at the Barefoot Bar on the beach, where you can chow down on burgers, fish, pizza, and salad. *Whalers Village, 2435 Kaanapali Pkwy.* ☎ *808/667-6636. www. hulagrill.com. Entrees $11–$18 in*

Barefoot Bar, $18–$35 in dining room. AE, DC, DISC, MC, V. Lunch & dinner daily. Map p 120.

★★ **Joe's Bar & Grill** WAILEA AMERICAN GRILL The 270-degree view of the golf course, tennis courts, ocean, and Haleakala is secondary to Chef Beverly Gannon's (see "Haliimaile General Store," p 124) American home cooking, from meatloaf to roasted portobello mushrooms. *Wailea Tennis Club, 131 Wailea Ike Place.* ☎ 808/875-7767. *Entrees $20–$42. AE, DC, DISC, MC, V. Dinner daily. Map p 122.*

Joy's Place KIHEI HEALTHY DELI/ SANDWICHES If you are in Kihei and are looking for a healthy, delicious lunch at a rock-bottom price, it's worth hunting around for this tiny hole in the wall with humongous sandwiches, fresh salads, hot soups, and yummy desserts. *Island Surf Bldg., 1993 S. Kihei Rd. (entrance to the restaurant is on Auhana St.).* ☎ 808/879-9258. *All items under $10. No credit cards. Mon–Sat 10am–5pm. Map p 122.*

★★★ **Ko** WAILEA GOURMET PLANTATION CUISINE The word ko means "cane," as in sugar cane, back to the old plantation days when the sugar-cane plantations had "camp" housing for each ethnic group and each had its own cuisine. There are wonderful taste treats you are only going to find here, so don't miss them. *Fairmont Kea Lani, 4100 Wailea Alanui Dr., Wailea.* ☎ 808/875-4100. *Entrees $28–$49. AE, DC, DISC, MC, V. Lunch & dinner daily. Map p 122.*

★★ kids **Kula Lodge** KULA HAWAII REGIONAL/ AMERICAN With huge breakfasts and awe-inspiring views, this upcountry lodge is a

Kula Lodge

must for visitors going up (or down) Haleakala. *Haleakala Hwy. (Hwy. 377).* ☎ 808/878-2517. *www.kula lodge.com. Entrees $12–$34. AE, DC, DISC, MC, V. Breakfast, lunch & dinner daily. Map p 119.*

★ kids **Lahaina Coolers** LAHAINA AMERICAN/INTERNATIONAL This ultracasual indoor/outdoor restaurant is a hangout for hungry surfers on a tight budget. *180 Dickensen St.* ☎ 808/661-7082. *www.lahaina coolers.com. Entrees $10–$24. AE, DC, DISC, MC, V. Breakfast, lunch & dinner daily. Map p 120.*

★★ kids **Lahaina Grill** LAHAINA NEW AMERICAN The chic flock to this hot spot for tequila shrimp with firecracker rice, Kona coffee–roasted rack of lamb, Maui onion–crusted seared *ahi*, and kalua duck quesadilla. There's a special kids' menu. *127 Lahainaluna Rd.* ☎ 808/667-5117. *www.lahaina grill.com. Entrees $36–$79. AE, DC, DISC, MC, V. Dinner daily. Map p 120.*

Seared ahi at Lahaina Grill.

Crusted ahi with asparagus at Mama's Fish House.

★★ **Longhi's** WAILEA *ITALIAN* The open-air room, black-and-white checkered floor, and yummy Italian cuisine (terrific breakfasts) make this an essential Wailea stop. *Shops at Wailea, 3750 Wailea Alanui Dr.* ☎ *808/891-8883. www.longhi-maui. com. Entrees $10–$80. AE, DC, MC, V. Breakfast, lunch & dinner daily. Map p 122.*

★★ **Mala Wailea** WAILEA *HAWAII REGIONAL CUISINE* Serving breakfast and wonderful dinners, this is

not to be missed as a food experience. Created by Chef Mark Ellman, one of the original founders of the Hawaiian Regional Cuisine movement, the restaurant offers island food in a very romantic atmosphere. *In the Wailea Beach Marriott Resort & Spa, 3700 Wailea Alanui Dr., Wailea.* ☎ *808/875-9394. www. malaoceantavern.com. Reservations recommended. Entrees $29–$44. AE, DC, DISC, MC, V. Breakfast & dinner daily. Map p 122.*

★★★ **Mama's Fish House** KUAU *SEAFOOD* On the beach, this South Seas fantasy worthy of Gauguin serves the most expensive (but worth it) fresh fish on Maui. *799 Poho Place, just off the Hana Hwy.* ☎ *808/579-8488. www.mamasfish house.com. Entrees $9–$25., DC, DISC, MC, V. Lunch & dinner daily. Map p 119.*

kids **Maui Tacos** NAPALI, LAHAINA, KIHEI, KAHULUI *MEXICAN* Hungry surfers, discerning diners, burrito buffs, and Hollywood glitterati flock to this fast, healthy, and cheap taco chain, where gourmet Mexican is served on paper plates.

Maui's Best Ice Cream: Roselani

Aloha ice cream aficionados: For the culinary experience of your trip, try **Roselani Ice Cream,** Maui's only made-from-scratch, old-fashioned ice cream. There are more than 40 different flavors to try, ranging from traditional vanilla to *haupia* (made from coconut and macadamia nut), or the popular chocolate macadamia nut, or Kona mud pie, or mango and cream, or coconut pineapple, or my favorite, luau fudge pie. For a list of hotels, restaurants, parlors, and grocery stores carrying Roselani, either call ☎ 808/244-7951 or check online at www.roselani.com.

Roselani's coconut ice cream.

Fresh seafood at the Pineapple Grill.

In Napili Plaza, 5095 Napili Hau St., ☎ 808/665-0222; Lahaina Square, 840 Wainee St., Lahaina, ☎ 808/661-8883; Kamaole Beach Center, 2411 S. Kihei Rd., Kihei; Queen Kaahumnau Center, 275 Kaahumanu Ave., Kahului., ☎ 808/871-7726. www.mauitacos.com. Items $3–$10. AE, DC, DISC, MC, V. Brunch, lunch & dinner daily. Map p 119, 120, 121, 122.

★ Milagros Food Company

PAIA *SOUTHWESTERN/SEAFOOD* Sit outdoors and watch the parade of people, from tie-died hippies to ultrachic Euros, as you tuck in at this casual eatery. Great margaritas. *Hana Hwy. and Baldwin Ave.* ☎ 808/579-8755. Breakfast items $7–$9; lunch items $10–$13; dinner entrees $15–$25. DC, MC, V. Breakfast, lunch & dinner daily. Map p 119.

★★ kids Moana Bakery & Cafe

PAIA *LOCAL/EUROPEAN* Paia's most creative cuisine, with Asian and European influences, highlights the menu at this stylish cafe. There's entertainment 3 nights a week, ranging from jazz to Hawaiian to Latin. *71 Baldwin Ave.* ☎ 808/579-9999. Entrees $9–$30. MC, V. Breakfast, lunch & dinner Tues–Sun; breakfast & lunch Mon. Map p 119.

kids Peggy Sue's KIHEI *AMERICAN* This 1950s-style diner has oodles of charm, with old-fashioned soda-shop stools and jukeboxes on every Formica table. You'll find shakes, floats, and egg creams, along with burgers, fries, and kids' meals for just $3.95. *Azeka Place II, 1279 S. Kihei Rd.* ☎ 808/875-8944. Burgers (with fries) $10–$12; lunch entrees $7–$9. AE, DISC, MC, V. Lunch & dinner daily. Map p 122.

★★★ Pineapple Grill Kapalua

KAPALUA *PACIFIC ISLAND* If you had only a single night to eat on the island of Maui, this would be the place to go. Up-and-coming young chef Ryan Luckey is winning high praise for his creative dishes from both critics and the locals who flock here nightly. *200 Kapalua Dr.* ☎ 808/669-9600. www.pineapple kapalua.com. Entrees $10–$40. AE, MC, V. Lunch & dinner daily. Map p 121.

★★ Roy's Kahana Bar & Grill

KAHANA *EURO-ASIAN* One of Hawaii's most successful restaurants, Roy's has no dramatic view and is upstairs in a shopping mall. Yet the fabulous food packs 'em in every night. *Kahana Gateway*

An entree at Roy's.

Shopping Center, 4405 Honoapiilani Hwy. ☎ 808/669-6999. www.roys restaurant.com. Entrees $6–$28. AE, DC, DISC, MC, V. Dinner daily. Map p 121.

★★ Sansei Seafood Restaurant and Sushi Bar KAPALUA & KIHEI *PACIFIC RIM* Perpetual award-winner Sansei offers an extensive menu of Japanese and East–West delicacies, which are part Pacific Rim, part Hawaii Regional. *Office Rd., Kapalua,* ☎ 808/669-6286, map p 121; *Kihei Town Center, Kihei,* ☎ 808/879-0004, map p 122. Entrees $19–$43. AE, DISC, MC, V. Dinner daily.

kids Shaka Sandwich & Pizza KIHEI *PIZZA* Award-winning pizzas, New York–style heroes, Philly cheese steaks, calzones, salads, just-baked garlic bread, and homemade meatball sandwiches, all with fresh Maui produce. *1770 S. Kihei Rd.* ☎ 808/874-0331. Entrees $7–$26. No credit cards. Lunch & dinner daily. Map p 122.

★ kids Stella Blues Cafe KIHEI *AMERICAN* There's something for everyone—vegetarians, kids, pasta and sandwich lovers, and hefty steak eaters—at this loud, lively, unpretentious eatery where Grateful Dead posters line the walls, and a covey of gleaming motorcycles is invariably parked outside. *Azeka II Shopping Center, 1279 S. Kihei Rd.* ☎ 808/874-3779. Entrees $6–$13 breakfast, $9–$13 lunch, $15–$28 dinner. AE, DC, DISC, MC, V. Breakfast, lunch & dinner daily. Map p 122.

★ kids Umalu WAILEA *PACIFIC RIM* This is the kind of restaurant that visitors dream about. *Umalu* translates into "the shade cast by a cliff" and that is a great description of the relaxed casual atmosphere of this outdoor oceanside restaurant. *In the Hyatt Regency Maui Resort & Spa, 200 Nohea Kai Dr., Kaanapali.* ☎ 808/661-1234. Entrees $13–$41. AE, DC, MC, V. Lunch & dinner daily. Map p 120.

★★ kids The Waterfront at Maalaea MAALAEA *SEAFOOD* The family-owned Waterfront has won many prestigious awards for service, the views, and, most of all, their just-caught seafood. *50 Hauoli St.* ☎ 808/244-9028. www.water frontrestaurant.net. Entrees $19–$38. AE, DC, DISC, MC, V. Dinner daily. Map p 122. ●

Sushi and sake at Sansei.

Shopping Best Bets

Best **Alohawear**
★★ Moonbow Tropics, *36 Baldwin Ave. (p 135)*

Best **Asian Antiques**
★ Brown-Kobayashi, *160-A N. Market St. (p 136)*

Best **Hawaiian Antiques**
★★ Bird of Paradise Unique Antiques, *56 N. Market St. (p 135)*

Best **Place to Browse**
★★★ Bailey House Museum Gift Shop, *2375-A Main St. (p 139)*

Best **Local Maui Artists**
★★★ Hana Coast Gallery, *In the Hotel Hana-Maui (p 136)*

Best **Cookies**
★★★ Broke da Mouth Cookies, *190 Alamaha St. (p 137)*

Best **Gifts**
★ Maui Crafts Guild, *43 Hana Hwy. (p 138)*

Best **Gifts for the Kids**
★★ Maui Ocean Center, *192 Maalaea Rd. (p 139)*

Best **Handblown Glass**
Ki'i Gallery, *Shops at Wailea (p 136)*

Best **High Fashion**
★★ Maggie Coulombe, *505 Front St. (p 138)*

Best **Place for a Lei**
Kmart, *424 Dairy Rd. (p 138)*

Best **Shoes**
★★★ Sandal Tree, *multiple locations (p 139)*

Best **Shopping Mall**
★ Queen Kaahumanu Center, *275 Kaahumanu Ave. (p 139)*

Best **Sinfully Delicious Bakery**
★ T. Komoda Store and Bakery, *3674 Baldwin Ave. (p 137)*

Best **Souvenir to Ship Home**
★★ Sunrise Protea, *Haleakala Hwy./Hwy. 37. (p 138)*

Best **Swimwear**
Lightning Bolt Maui, *55 Kaahumanu Ave. (p 135)*

Best **T-Shirt Selection**
Crazy Shirts, *multiple locations (p 140)*

The Maui Ocean Center has great gifts for kids.

Maui & Paia Shopping

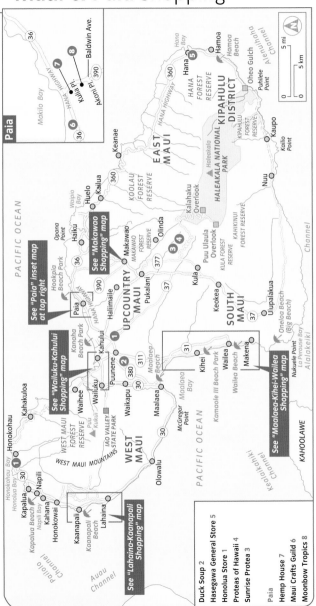

Duck Soup 2

Hasegawa General Store 5

Honolua Store 1

Proteas of Hawaii 4

Sunrise Protea 3

Paia

Hemp House 7

Maui Crafts Guild 6

Moonbow Tropics 8

Photo p 129: Colorful leis for sale.

Lahaina & Kaanapali Shopping

Crazy Shirts (Lahaina) 6
Crazy Shirts (Lahaina Cannery Mall) 3
Crazy Shirts (Whaler's Village) 1
Crazy Shirts (Wharf Cinema) 8
Ki'i Gallery 2
Lahaina Arts Society Galleries 9
Lahaina Cannery Mall 3
Lahaina Center 4
Maggie Coulombe 10
The Old Lahaina Book Emporium 5
Paul Ropp 1
Sandal Tree (Hyatt Regency Maui) 2
Sandal Tree (Whaler's Village) 1
Village Galleries in Lahaina 7
Whaler's Village 1

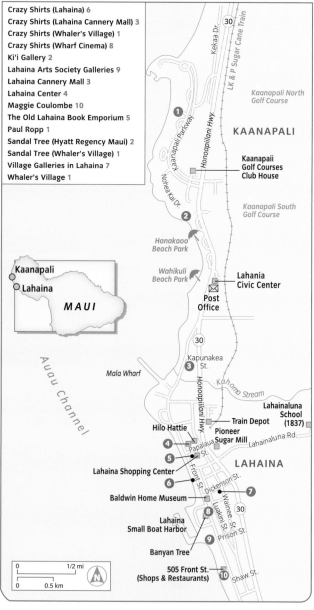

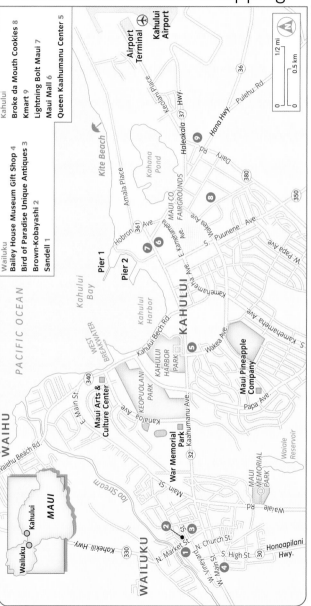

Wailuku & Kahului Shopping

Wailuku
Bailey House Museum Gift Shop 4
Bird of Paradise Unique Antiques 3
Brown-Kobayashi 2
Sandell 1

Kahului
Broke da Mouth Cookies 8
Kmart 9
Lightning Bolt Maui 7
Maui Mall 6
Queen Kaahumanu Center 5

Maalaea/Kihei/Wailea Shopping

Crazy Shirts
(Piilani Village Shopping Center) 2
Crazy Shirts
(The Shops at Wailea) 3
CY Maui 3
Ki'i (Grand Wailea Resort) 4
Ki'i (The Shops at Wailea) 3
Maui Ocean Center 1
Sandal Tree 4
The Shops at Wailea 3

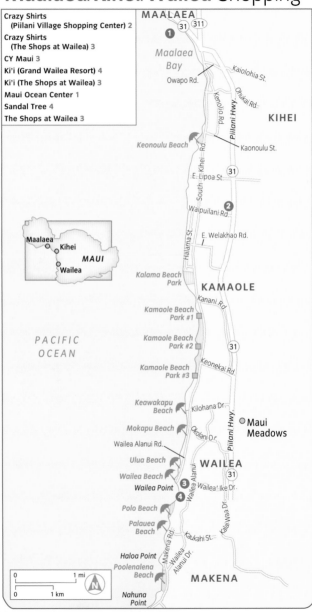

MAALAEA

Maalaea Bay

Kaiolohia St.

Owapo Rd.

Piilani Hwy.

Ohukai Rd.

Kenolio Rd.

KIHEI

Keonoulu Beach

South Kihei Rd.

Kaonoulu St.

E. Lipoa St.

Waipuilani Rd.

Halama St.

E. Welakhao Rd.

Kalama Beach Park

KAMAOLE

Kanani Rd.

Kamaole Beach Park #1

Kamaole Beach Park #2

Keonekai Rd.

PACIFIC OCEAN

Kamaole Beach Park #3

Keawakapu Beach

Kilohana Dr.

Mokapu Beach

Okolani Dr.

Piilani Hwy.

Maui Meadows

Wailea Alanui Rd.

Ulua Beach

WAILEA

Wailea Beach

Wailea Alanui

Wailea Point

Wailea 'Ike Dr.

Polo Beach

Kalai Waa Dr.

Palauea Beach

Makena Rd.

Kaukahi St.

Haloa Point

Wailea Alanui Dr.

Poolenalena Beach

MAKENA

Nahuna Point

Maalaea

Kihei

MAUI

Wailea

0   1 mi
0   1 km

Makawao Shopping

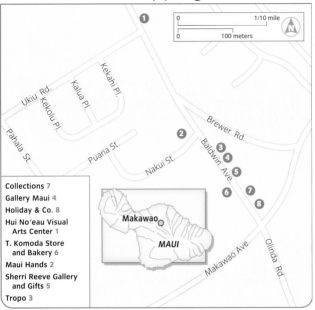

0	1/10 mile
0	100 meters

Collections **7**
Gallery Maui **4**
Holiday & Co. **8**
Hui No'eau Visual
  Arts Center **1**
T. Komoda Store
  and Bakery **6**
Maui Hands **2**
Sherri Reeve Gallery
  and Gifts **5**
Tropo **3**

Maui Shopping A to Z

Alohawear
kids Lightning Bolt Maui Inc.
KAHULUI I love the excellent selection of women's board shorts, aloha shirts, swimwear, sandals, and shoes, and all the necessary accoutrements for fun in the sun. *55 Kaahumanu Ave.* ☎ *808/877-3484. AE, DC, MC, V. Map p 133.*

★★ Moonbow Tropics PAIA
I've found some top label aloha shirts here. *36 Baldwin Ave.* ☎ *808/ 579-8592. AE, DISC, MC, V. Map p 131.*

Tropo MAKAWAO A good stop for stylish men's aloha wear. *3643 Baldwin Ave.* ☎ *808/573-0356. AE, MC, V. Map p 135.*

Antiques & Collectibles
★★ Bird of Paradise Unique Antiques WAILUKU I love wandering through the Hawaiiana

A display of Moonbow Tropics shirts.

nostalgia here. Items range from 1940s rattan furniture to vintage aloha shirts and classic Hawaiian music on cassettes. *56 N. Market St.* ☎ *808/242-7699. AE, MC, V. Map p 133.*

★ **Brown-Kobayashi** WAILUKU The focus is gracious living with Asian antiques. You'll find Japanese kimonos and obi, exotic Chinese woods, and more. *160-A N. Market St.* ☎ *808/242-0804. AE, MC, V. Map p 133.*

Duck Soup PUUNENE I've found terrific deals on jewelry, handbags, and artwork at this virtually unknown warehouse full of Asian and Indonesian treasures. It's a bit out-of-the-way; call for directions. *Off Hwy. 311, about a mile from Puunene, near the Maui Animal Shelter and the Central Maui Baseyard.* ☎ *808/871-7875. MC, V. Map p 131.*

Art—Hawaiian

Gallery Maui MAKAWAO Pop in to see the quality of work by Maui artists, from Norfolk pine bowls to watercolors. *3643-A Baldwin Ave.* ☎ *808/572-8092. AE, DC, MC, V. Map p 135.*

★★★ **Hana Coast Gallery** HANA If you go to only one gallery, make it this award-winning one devoted entirely to Hawaii's top artists (sculptures, paintings, prints, feather work, stonework, and carvings). It's Maui's best selection under one roof. *In the Hotel Hana-Maui.* ☎ *808/248-8636. AE, MC, V. Map p 109.*

★★ **Hui No'eau Visual Arts Center** MAKAWAO I can spend hours wandering the gift shop, which features many one-of-a-kind local works. *2841 Baldwin Ave.* ☎ *808/572-6560. www.huinoeau. com. AE, DISC, MC, V. Map p 135.*

Ki'i Gallery KAANAPALI, WAILEA This shop features glass in all forms, from handblown vessels to jewelry. I can't pass by without stopping to browse. *In the Hyatt Regency Maui, 200 Nohea Kai Dr.,* ☎ *808/661-4456, map p 132; the Grand Wailea Resort,* ☎ *808/874-3059, map p 134; Shops at Wailea,* ☎ *808/874-1181, map p 134. AE, DC, DISC, MC, V.*

★★ **Lahaina Arts Society Galleries** LAHAINA Changing monthly exhibits of the Maui artist-members

Glass display at Ki'i Gallery.

A painting at the Sherri Reeve Gallery.

range from paintings to fiber art, to ceramics, sculpture, prints, jewelry, and more. Art in the Park fairs are every second and fourth weekend of the month. *648 Wharf St.* ☎ *808/661-3228. MC, V. Map p 132.*

★ **Sherri Reeve Gallery and Gifts** MAKAWAO If you want to take a bit of the vibrant color and feel of the islands home with you, stop by this open-air gallery that sells everything from inexpensive cards, hand-painted tiles, and T-shirts to original works and limited editions. *3669 Baldwin Ave.* ☎ *808/572-8931. www.sreeve.com. AE, DISC, MC, V. Map p 135.*

Village Galleries in Lahaina LAHAINA The oldest continuously operated gallery on Maui is known among art collectors as a showcase for regional artists. *120 and 180 Dickenson St.* ☎ *808/661-4402 or 808/661-5559. Also at the Ritz-Carlton Kapalua, 1 Ritz-Carlton Dr.* ☎ *808/669-1800. Map p 132.*

Bookstores
The Old Lahaina Book Emporium LAHAINA Chockablock with 25,000 used books in stacks, shelves, counters, and aisles, this bookstore is a browser's dream. It has great books on Hawaii. *834 Front St.* ☎ *808/661-1399. Map p 132.*

Edibles
★★★ **kids** **Broke da Mouth Cookies** KAHULUI This store is my weakness: terrific cookies ($3.25 a bag), ranging from chocolate mac-nut, oatmeal raisin, and shortbread to almond, peanut butter, and coconut crunch. So good, you'll eat them long before you get home. *190 Alamaha St.* ☎ *808/873-9255. No credit cards. Map p 133.*

★ **kids** **T. Komoda Store and Bakery** MAKAWAO Get here early before their famous cream puffs are sold out; also check out the delicious cinnamon rolls, doughnuts, pies, and chocolate cake. *3674 Baldwin Ave.* ☎ *808/572-7261. No credit cards. Map p 135.*

Fashion
★ **Collections** MAKAWAO One of my favorites, this eclectic shop is filled with spirited clothing reflecting the ease and color of island living. *3677 Baldwin Ave.* ☎ *808/572-0781. MC, V. Map p 135.*

CY Maui WAILEA Women looking for washable, flowing clothing in silks, rayons, and natural fibers will love this shop. *In Shops at Wailea, 3750 Wailea Alanui Dr., A-30.* ☎ *808/891-0782. AE, MC, V. Map p 134.*

Hemp House PAIA A surprisingly great selection of clothing and accessories made of hemp (jeans, linenlike pants, dresses, shirts, and so on), a sturdy, ecofriendly, and sensible fiber. *16 Baldwin Ave.* ☎ *808/579-8880. AE, DISC, MC, V. Map p 131.*

★ **Holiday & Co.** MAKAWAO I love to just wander around this tiny store checking out the collection of surprisingly attractive natural fiber women's clothing, ranging from easygoing dresses to shawls, even a few aloha shirts. *3681 Baldwin Ave.* ☎ *808/572-1470. AE, DC, DISC, MC, V. Map p 135.*

The interior of Maggie Coulombe.

★★ Maggie Coulombe LAHAINA I cannot resist this high-fashion store with Maggie Coulombe's latest couture, jersey, linen, pareo, and shoes, plus accessories, jewelry, and a few surprises. *505 Front St.* ☎ *808/662-0696. www.maggiecoulombe.com. AE, DC, DISC, MC, V. Map p 132.*

Paul Ropp KAANAPALI The Bali fashion designer's only store outside of Indonesia features his lively, colorful, and eccentric style of dressing, which is perfect for Maui's tropical climate. *In Whalers Village, 2435 Kaanapali Pkwy.* ☎ *808/661-8000. AE, DISC, MC, V. Map p 132.*

Flowers & Leis
Kmart KAHALUI I've scoured the island and, surprisingly, this chain store has some of the most unusual and outstanding leis on Maui at very moderate prices. *424 Dairy Rd.* ☎ *808/871-8553. AE, DISC, MC, V. Map p 133.*

Proteas of Hawaii KULA In addition to flowers, this store offers regular walking tours of the University of Hawaii Extension Service gardens across the street. *417 Mauna Place.* ☎ *808/878-2533. www.proteasof hawaii.com. MC, V. Map p 131.*

★★ Sunrise Protea KULA Send these other-worldly flowers back home to your friends—not only will they survive shipping anywhere in the world, but your pals will also be astounded and amazed. *Haleakala Hwy./Hwy. 37.* ☎ *808/876-0200. www.sunriseprotea.com. AE, DISC, MC, V. Map p 131.*

General Stores
★★ Hasegawa General Store HANA I love this old-fashioned store, where the aisles are choked with merchandise from groceries to every tape and CD that mentions Hana, and even T-shirts and beach toys. *Hana Hwy., in Hana.* ☎ *808/248-8231. AE, MC, V. Map p 131.*

★★ Honolua Store KAPALUA For the best prices in a pricey resort area, this is my favorite place to get every day essentials, clothing, even budget-priced deli items. *502 Office Rd.* ☎ *808/669-6128. AE, DC, DISC, MC, V. Map p 131.*

Hawaiian Gifts
★ Maui Crafts Guild PAIA The high quality and unique artwork at this artist-owned and -operated guild encompasses everything from pit-fired raku to hand-painted fabrics,

jewelry, beadwork, traditional Hawaiian stonework, and even banana bark paintings. *43 Hana Hwy.* ☎ *808/579-9697. AE, MC, V. Map p 131.*

Maui Hands MAKAWAO Great Hawaiian gifts can be found at this store, where 90% of the items are made by Maui artists and sold at prices that aren't inflated. *Courtyard, 3620 Baldwin Ave.* ☎ *808/572-5194 or 808/579-9245. AE, MC, V. Map p 135.*

Museum Stores

★★★ **Bailey House Museum Gift Shop** WAILUKU For made-in-Hawaii items, this small shop is a must stop. The selection of remarkable gift items includes Hawaiian music, exquisite woods, traditional Hawaiian games, pareus, books, *lauhala* hats, hand-sewn pheasant hatbands, jams and jellies, Maui cookbooks, and an occasional Hawaiian quilt. *2375-A Main St.* ☎ *808/244-3326. MC, V. Map p 133.*

★★ kids **Maui Ocean Center** MAALAEA Stop here for plush stuffed marine animals; nature books; T-shirts; and an array of fine artwork, jewelry, and Hawaiiana created by some of the island's most prominent artists. *Maalaea Harbor Village, 192 Maalaea Rd. (the triangle btw. Honoapiilani Hwy. and Maalaea Rd.).* ☎ *808/270-7000. AE, DISC, MC, V. Map p 134.*

Shoes

★★★ **Sandal Tree** KAANAPALI, WAILEA My fave store for sandals, ranging from rubber thongs, athletic shoes, and Top-Siders to dressy pumps, designer footwear, hats, and much more. Prices are realistic too. *In Whalers Village, 2435 Kaanapali Pkwy.* ☎ *808/667-5330, map p 132; in Grand Wailea Resort, 3850 Wailea Alanui Dr., Wailea,*

☎ *808/874-9006, map p 134; in Hyatt Regency Maui, 200 Nohea Kai Dr.,* ☎ *808/661-3495, map p 132. AE, MC, V.*

Shopping Centers

Lahaina Cannery Mall LAHAINA This former pineapple cannery is now a maze of shops and restaurants. Check out Sir Wilfred's Coffee House, where you can unwind with espresso and croissants. *1221 Honoapiilani Hwy., Lahaina.* ☎ *808/661-5304. Map p 132.*

Lahaina Center LAHAINA Still a work in progress, this mall has easy access to more than 30 shops, a salon, restaurants, a nightclub, and a four-plex movie-theater complex. *900 Front St.* ☎ *808/667-9216. Map p 132.*

Maui Mall KAHULUI This is a place for daily shopping with stores like Longs Drugs and Star Market. Don't miss **Tasaka Guri Guri,** a decades-old purveyor of icy treats. *70 E. Kaahumanu Ave.* ☎ *808/877-7559. Map p 133.*

★ kids **Queen Kaahumanu Center** KAHULUI Offers more

A fish plate at the Maui Ocean Center's gift shop.

than 100 shops, restaurants, and theaters. Kaahumanu covers all the bases, from arts and crafts to a **Foodland Supermarket.** *275 Kaahumanu Ave.* ☎ *808/877-3369. Map p 133.*

★ **The Shops at Wailea** WAILEA This collection of high-end shops sells expensive souvenirs, gifts, clothing, and accessories. The chains rule, but dedicated shoppers can still find some more unusual options. My picks include **Na Hoku,** *the* place to go for creative, distinctive jewelry with an island touch; and **Ki`i Gallery,** which houses one of Hawaii's most comprehensive collections of fine art from glass to original paintings. *3750 Wailea Alanui.* ☎ *808/891-6770. www. shopsatwailea.com. Map p 134.*

Calla lily vases at Ki`i Gallery.

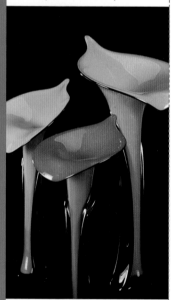

Shopping Tip

Shopping in resort areas, especially Lahaina or Kaanapali, can be expensive, as parking lots charge anywhere from $3 an hour to $7 a day. If you are set on parking either at the Lahaina Center or Whalers Village, pick up a copy of the free magazine *This Week Maui* and clip their free parking coupons.

Whalers Village Kaanapali   I find upscale Whalers Village disappointing. Although it offers everything from Prada to Ferragamo, it's short on local shops, and parking at the nearby lot is expensive. The only stores I recommend are **Lahaina Printsellers, Cinnamon Girl,** and **Paul Ropp** (p 138). *2435 Kaanapali Pkwy.* ☎ *808/661-4567. Map p 132.*

T-Shirts

★★ **Crazy Shirts** VARIOUS LOCATIONS   Confession: A huge portion of my wardrobe consists of Crazy Shirts T-shirts. These 100% cotton T-shirts not only last for years, but they also make perfect souvenirs and gifts. *Whalers Village,* ☎ *808/ 661-0117, map p 132; 865 Front St.,* ☎ *808/661-4775, map p 132; Wharf Cinema,* ☎ *808/661-4712, map p 132; Piilani Village Shopping Center,* ☎ *808/875-6440, map p 134; Lahaina Cannery Mall,* ☎ *808/661-4788, map p 132; Shops at Wailea,* ☎ *808/875-6435, map p 134. AE, DISC, MC, V.*

Sandell WAILUKU   If you want the inside scoop on Maui politics as well as some social commentary, stop by and chat with artist-illustrator-cartoonist David Sandell, who has provided insight on Maui since the early 1970s through his artwork. Also check out his inexpensive T-shirts. *133 Market St.* ☎ *808/249-0234. No credit cards. Map p 133.* ●

Nightlife & Performing Arts
Best Bets

Best Place to Bury Your Toes in the Sand
★ Leilani's/Hula Grill, *Whalers Village* (p 145)

Best for Hawaiian Music
★★ Hapa's Night Club, *41 E. Lipoa St.* (p 145)

Best Dance Floor
★★ Casanova, *1188 Makawao Ave.* (p 145)

Best Place to Drink with Locals
★ Kahului Ale House, *355 E. Kamehameha Ave.* (p 145)

Best Family Show
★★★ kids Kupanaha, *Kaanapali Beach Hotel* (p 146)

Best Music
★★ kids Moanai Bakery & Café, *71 Baldwin Ave.* (p 146)

Best Hawaiian Slack-Key Music
★★★ kids Masters of Hawaiian Slack-Key Guitar Series, *Napili Kai Beach Resort* (p 147)

Best Hotel Lounge
★ Four Seasons Lobby Lounge, *Four Seasons Wailea* (p 145)

Best Luau
★★★ kids Old Lahaina Luau, *1251 Front St.* (p 148)

Best Performing Arts Center
★★★ Maui Arts and Cultural Center, *1 Cameron Way* (p 146)

Best for Big Name Musicians
★★ Casanova, *1188 Makawao Ave.* (p 145)

Best Show
★★★ kids 'Ulalena, *878 Front St.* (p 146)

Best for Movies
★★★ Maui Film Festival, *Wailea Golf Course* (p 145)

Enjoy a cocktail with your Maui sunset.

Sunset Cocktails

At the southern end of Lahaina, in the 505 Front St. complex, **Pacific'o** (☎ 808/667-4341) is a solid hit, with a raised bar, seating on the ocean, and a backdrop of Lanai across the channel. A few steps away sister restaurant **I'o** shares the same vista, with an appetizer menu and a techno-curved bar that will wow you as much as the drop-dead-gorgeous view.

In Wailea, the restaurants at the new Shops at Wailea (3750 Wailea Alanui), including highly successful **Tommy Bahama** (☎ 808/875-9983) and **Longhi's** (☎ 808/891-8883), are a noteworthy addition to the sunset scene.

Maui/Wailuku/Kahului Nightlife

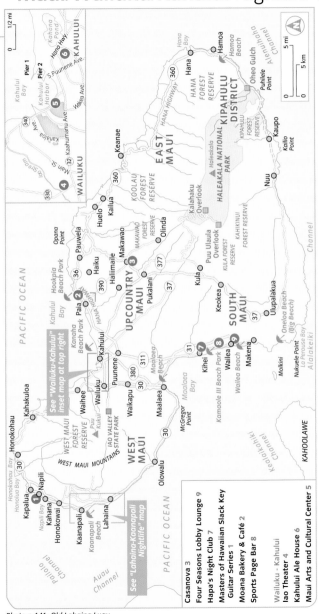

Casanova 3
Four Seasons Lobby Lounge 9
Hapa's Night Club 7
Masters of Hawaiian Slack Key
Guitar Series 1
Moana Bakery & Café 2
Sports Page Bar 8

Wailuku - Kahului
Iao Theater 4
Kahului Ale House 6
Maui Arts and Cultural Center 5

Photo p 141: Old Lahaina Luau.

Lahaina & Kaanapali Nightlife

Cheeseburger in Paradise 7
Feast at Lele 8
Hard Rock Café 4
Kupanaha 1
Leilani's/Hula Grill 2
Longhi's 5
Maui Brews 4
Old Lahaina Luau 3
'Ulalena 6
Warren & Annabelle's 4

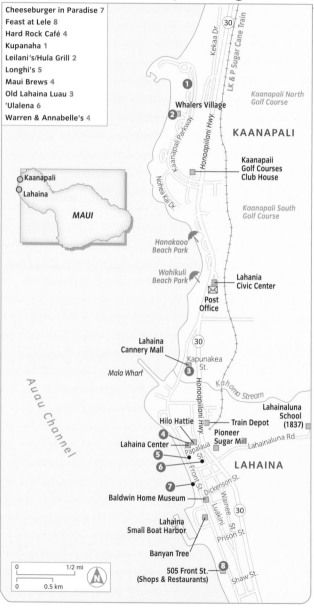

Kekaa Dr.

LK & P Sugar Cane Train

Kaanapali North
Golf Course

Whalers Village

KAANAPALI

Honoapiilani Hwy.

Kaanapali Parkway

Kaanapali
Golf Courses
Club House

Nohea Kai Dr.

Kaanapali South
Golf Course

Hanakaoo
Beach Park

Wahikuli
Beach Park

Lahaina
Civic Center

Post
Office

Kaanapali
Lahaina

MAUI

Lahaina
Cannery Mall

Kapunakea
St.

Mala Wharf

Honoapiilani Hwy.

Kahoma Stream

Lahainaluna
School
(1837)

Auau Channel

Hilo Hattie

Train Depot

Lahaina Center

Pioneer
Sugar Mill

Lahainaluna Rd.

Papalaua St.

Front St.

LAHAINA

Dickenson St.

Baldwin Home Museum

Wainee St.

Luakini St.

Prison St.

30

Lahaina
Small Boat Harbor

Banyan Tree

505 Front St.
(Shops & Restaurants)

Shaw St.

0   1/2 mi
0   0.5 km

Maui Nightlife A to Z

Bars & Cocktail Lounges
★★ Casanova MAKAWAO
Expect good blues, rock 'n' roll, reggae, jazz, Hawaiian, and the top names in local and visiting entertainment. I love the Sunday afternoon live jazz from 3 to 6pm. *1188 Makawao Ave.* ☎ *808/572-0220. Map p 143.*

Cheeseburger in Paradise
LAHAINA   Loud, live tropical rock blasts into the streets and out to sea nightly from 4:30 to 11pm. *Front/Lahainaluna sts.* ☎ *808/661-4855. Map p 144.*

★ Four Seasons Lobby Lounge
WAILEA   For a quiet evening with gentle jazz or soft Hawaiian music, sink into the plush furniture and order an exotic drink. Nightly live music from 8:30 to 11:30pm. *Four Seasons Wailea.* ☎ *808/874-8000. Map p 143.*

★★ Hapa's Night Club KIHEI
When I'm hungry for the sweet sounds of Hawaiian music, I give Hapa's a call to see who's on for the night. *41 E. Lipoa St.* ☎ *808/879-9001. Map p 143.*

Hard Rock Cafe LAHAINA   DJs (and occasional live music) entertain at this loud, 20-something scene.

Enjoy movies under the stars in the Celestial Cinema.

900 Front St. ☎ *808/667-7400. Map p 144.*

★ Kahului Ale House KAHULUI
Locals gather here for karaoke and live music. A DJ spins on Saturday from 10pm. *355 E. Kamehameha Ave.* ☎ *808/877-9001. Map p 143.*

★ Leilani's/Hula Grill KAANA-
PALI   Both oceanfront restaurants have busy, upbeat bars and tables

Maui Movie Magic

If you are headed to Maui, try to plan your trip around the Maui Film Festival (☎ 808/579-9244; www.mauifilmfestival.com), which always starts the Wednesday before Father's Day in June. The 5-day festival premiers films nightly in the Celestial Cinema, an under-the-stars, open-air outdoor theater on the Wailea Golf Course, which features a 50-foot-wide (15m) screen in Dolby Digital Surround Sound.

on the sand. Hula Grill's Barefoot Bar appetizer menu is a cut above Leilani's. Leilani's has live music daily from 3:30 to 6pm, while at Hula Grill the happy hour starts at 3pm and the live music at 6pm. *Whalers Village. Leilani's* ☎ *808/661-4495. Hula Grill* ☎ *808/667-6636. Map p 144.*

Longhi's LAHAINA Live salsa or jazz spills out into the streets from 9:30pm on weekends. I love people-watching here. It's a real mix, with everyone from Midwestern tourists to the occasional rock star. *888 Front St.* ☎ *808/667-2288. Map p 144.*

Maui Brews LAHAINA A young, hip crowd comes to this late-night restaurant-turned nightclub after 9pm, for the swing, salsa, reggae, and jams—either live or with a DJ. *900 Front St.* ☎ *808/667-7794. Map p 144.*

★★ **kids Moanai Bakery & Café** PAIA This retro restaurant is my favorite place to relax. Bring the entire family for the Vintage Hawaiian 6:30 to 9pm on Wednesday, smooth jazz and hot blues 6:30 to 9pm on Friday, and flamingo guitar and gypsy violin 6 to 9pm on Sunday. *71 Baldwin Ave.* ☎ *808/579-9999. Map p 143.*

Sports Page Bar KIHEI This crowded, typical sports bar features live music Monday through Saturday from 9pm. *2411 S. Kihei Rd.* ☎ *808/879-0602. Map p 143.*

Dance, Theater & Shows

Iao Theater WAILUKU It's not Broadway, but Maui does have live community theater, ranging from locally written productions to well-known plays and musicals. *68 N. Market St.,* ☎ *808/244-8680 or 808/242-6969 for box office and program information. www.mauionstage.com. Map p 143.*

★★★ **kids Kupanaha** KAANAPALI This dinner show for the entire family, which features magic, illusions, and the story of the Hawaii fire goddess, Pele, gets my vote for a great family outing. Tuesday through Saturday from 5 to 8pm. *In the Kaanapali Beach Hotel.* ☎ *808/661-0011. www.kbhmaui.com. Tickets (which include dinner) $82–$92 adults, $57 ages 13–20, $41 ages 6–12, free for ages 5 and under. Map p 144.*

★★★ **Maui Arts and Cultural Center** KAHULUI This is a first-class center for the visual and performing arts. Bonnie Raitt has performed here, as have Pearl Jam, Ziggy Marley, Tony Bennett, the American Indian Dance Theatre, the Maui Symphony Orchestra, and Jonny Lang, not to mention the finest in local talent. The center has a visual-arts gallery, an outdoor amphitheater, and two theaters. *1 Cameron Way.* ☎ *808/242-7469. www.mauiarts.org. Ticket prices vary. Map p 143.*

★★★ **kids 'Ulalena** LAHAINA The whole family will be riveted by this incredible show which weaves Hawaiian mythology with drama,

Maui Arts and Cultural Center.

Slack-key master and two-time Grammy winner, Keoki Kahumoku.

dance, and state-of-the-art multimedia. The cast performs Polynesian dance, original music, acrobatics, and chant in an interactive experience that often leaves the audience breathless. *Maui Myth and Magic Theatre, 878 Front St.* ☎ *877/688-4800 or 808/661-9913. www.ulalena.com. Tues–Sat 6:30pm. Tickets $60–$130 adults, $40–$85 children 12 and under. Map p 144.*

★ Warren & Annabelle's

LAHAINA   This unusual magic/comedy cocktail show stars illusionist Warren Gibson and "Annabelle," a ghost from the 1800s. She plays the grand piano as Warren dazzles you with his sleight-of-hand magic. *900 Front St.* ☎ *808/667-6244. www. warrenandannabelles.com. Tickets $56–$95. Map p 144.*

Hawaiian Music

★★★ kids Masters of Hawaiian Slack-Key Guitar Series NAPILI

For a chance to see a side of Hawaii that few visitors do, come to this Wednesday night production, where host George Kahumoku, Jr., introduces a new slack-key master every week. Not only is there incredible Hawaiian music and singing, but George and his guest also "talk story" about old Hawaii, music, and Hawaiian culture. *In the Napili Kai Beach Resort.* ☎ *888/669-3858. www.slackkey.com. Tickets $46. Map p 143.*

Entertainment at the Old Lahaina Luau.

Live music at the Hula Grill (p 145).

Luau

★★★ kids Old Lahaina Luau

LAHAINA   This is the best luau on Maui—perhaps in the entire state. The luau begins at sunset and features Tahitian and Hawaiian entertainment, including ancient hula, modern hula, and an intelligent narrative on the dance's rocky course of survival into modern times. The entertainment is riveting. The food, served from an open-air thatched structure, is as much Pacific Rim as Hawaiian, and mixes in some well-known western favorites. If you have been here, then be sure to see the **Feast at Lele** (p 123). *1251 Front St.* ☎ *800/248-5828 or 808/667-1998. www.oldlahainaluau.com. Tickets $96 adults, $65 children 12 and under. Map p 144.* ●

The Best of Lanai **in One Day**

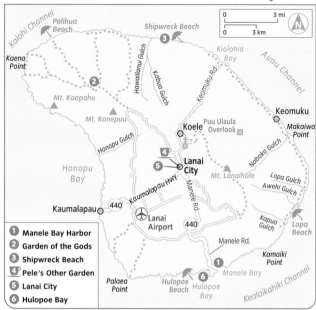

1. **Manele Bay Harbor**
2. **Garden of the Gods**
3. **Shipwreck Beach**
4. **Pele's Other Garden**
5. **Lanai City**
6. **Hulopoe Bay**

The smallest of all the Hawaiian Islands, Lanai was once a big pineapple plantation. Today it is home to two exclusive resorts, hundreds of years of history, one small town, and some of the friendliest people you will ever meet. It's possible to get an overview of this island in a single day: If you catch the first ferry, departing at 6:45am, you can see all my favorite spots (the island's unusual "supernatural" site, a windswept beach that's perfect for beachcombing, and quaint Lanai City), plus get in some beach time and still make it back to Lahaina in time for dinner. START: **Manele Bay Harbor. Trip length: 68 miles (109km).**

1 Manele Bay Harbor. To make the most of your day on Lanai, take the first ferry, which leaves at 6:45am. Seeing the morning sunlight glinting off the ocean is one of my favorite ways to start the day. Small, picturesque Manele Bay Harbor has a handful of boats ranging from old fishing vessels to luxury

Previous page: Two people relaxing on Hulopoe Beach.

high-tech yachts. If you've already arranged a 4-wheel-drive rental through the ferry company (p 152), they'll pick you up at the harbor and take you to the car-rental company in Lanai City, a 30- to 40-minute trip.

From the car-rental company in Lanai City, it's another 14 miles (23km) to the Garden of the Gods. Turn right onto Lanai Avenue,

Manele Bay Harbor.

then left (north) to Hwy. 430 (Keomuku Hwy.). Turn left on Poliha Road, just behind the stables and before the tennis courts (look for the rock sign that says GARDEN OF THE GODS). Allow about 25 minutes.

2 ★★ **kids Garden of the Gods.** Allow about 15 minutes to explore this rugged, barren, beautiful place on Lanai's north shore. You'll arrive early in the morning, when the light casts eerie shadows on these mysterious lava formations. Strewn by volcanic forces, the rocks are a brilliant mix of reds, oranges, ochers, and yellows. Ancient Hawaiians considered this desolate, windswept place supernatural. Scientists, however, have other, less colorful explanations. Some call the area an "ongoing

Garden of the Gods.

posterosional event"; others say it's just "plain and simple badlands."

Retrace your steps to Hwy. 430 (Keomuku Hwy.) and turn left. Continue down the steep switchback to the ocean. Turn left and drive to the end of the road. Allow 60 minutes to drive these 20 miles (32km) on windy, dirt roads.

3 ★ **kids Shipwreck Beach.** This 8-mile-long (13km) windswept strand on Lanai's northeastern shore—named for the rusty ship *Liberty* stuck on the coral reef—is a sailor's nightmare and a beachcomber's dream. The swimming isn't great here, nor is the snorkeling (too murky), but this is the best place in Hawaii to beachcomb. Strong currents yield all sorts of flotsam, from Japanese handblown-glass fish floats and rare pelagic paper nautilus shells to lots of junk. From December to April, when the Pacific humpbacks cruise in from Alaska, this is also a great place to spot whales. Plan to spend about an hour.

It will take about 45 minutes to retrace your route back up Hwy. 430, into Lanai City, 12 miles (19km) away. Continue down Lanai Avenue, turn right on

Getting To & Around Lanai

There are no direct flights from the mainland to Lanai; you'll have to make a connection in Honolulu or Kahului (on Maui), where you catch a plane for the 25-minute flight to Lanai's airport. Twin-engine planes are the only air service to Lanai. **PW Express** (☎ 888/866-5022 or 808/873-0877; www.pacificwings.com), offers daily nonstop flights between Lanai and Honolulu. Another inexpensive air carrier is **Mokulele Airlines** (☎ 868/260-7070; www.mokuleleairlines.com). Also offering service to Lanai is **Island Air** (☎ 800/323-3345 from the mainland, 800/652-6541 interisland, or 808/565-6744; www.islandair.com), with daily flights from Honolulu. I must tell you, however, that I have gotten less than sterling service from Island Air, which has left me stranded midroute—not once, but twice!

Another option is a round-trip on **Expeditions Lahaina/Lanai Passenger Ferry** (☎ 808/661-3756; www.go-lanai.com), which costs $52 for adults and $42 for children. The ferry runs five times daily between Lahaina Harbor and Lanai's Manele Bay Harbor. The 9-mile (14km) channel crossing takes 45 minutes to an hour, depending on sea conditions. Reservations are strongly recommended. Baggage is limited to two checked bags and one carry-on.

I recommend renting a 4-wheel-drive vehicle to use on the island. (Lanai only has 30 miles/48km of paved roads, and hundreds of miles of unpaved roads.) You can book through Expeditions; the $176 rental fee includes a round-trip ferry ticket for one.

Pele's Other Garden.

Hulopoe Beach.

Eighth Avenue, just after Dole Square. Park next to the Square on Eighth across from Houston Street.

4 ★★ kids **Pele's Other Garden.** This deli and bistro is a good lunch spot. You can take out, but I love to order one of their wraps and sit outside under one of the umbrellas, watching the goings-on in the town square. See p 158.

5 ★★ kids **Lanai City.** Perched at 1,645 feet (501m) above sea level, almost at the dead center of the island, sits this old-fashioned town centered on Dole Square. Built in 1924, this plantation village is a tidy grid of quaint tin-roofed cottages in bright pastels, with tropical gardens of banana, *lilikoi,* and papaya. The charming village square is lined with towering Norfolk and Cook Island pines and plantation buildings housing a couple of general stores selling basic necessities, a smattering of restaurants, an art

gallery, an art center, and a whimsical shop. A few blocks over is a post office and a coffee shop that outshines any Starbucks. Give yourself an hour or two to mosey from one shop to the next.

Continue down Eighth Avenue to Fraser Avenue and turn left. Go right at Hwy. 440 (Kaumalapau Hwy.). Turn left at Manele Road, where Hwy. 440 continues. Continue to the end at Hulupoe Beach Park. Allow 30 to 35 minutes for the 11-mile (18km) trip.

6 ★★★ kids **Hulopoe Beach.** This wide beach is one of my favorites in the entire state. Not only is it a terrific snorkeling spot (especially along the rocks to your left as you face the ocean), but it is also a marine preserve, where taking of fish or other marine critters is forbidden. Boats cannot anchor in the bay, so you have the entire ocean to yourself.

Take the 5-minute walk from Hulopoe Beach Park to Manele Bay to catch the last ferry back to Lahaina at 6:45pm.

The Best of Lanai **in Three Days**

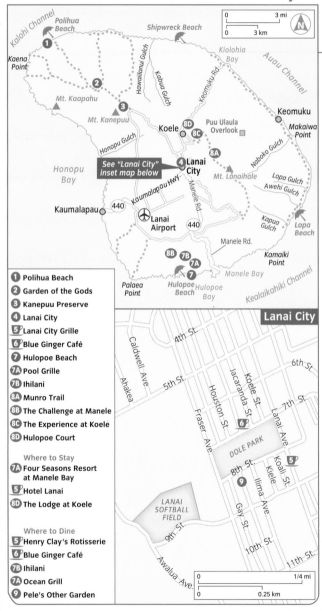

1 Polihua Beach
2 Garden of the Gods
3 Kanepuu Preserve
4 Lanai City
5 Lanai City Grille
6 Blue Ginger Café
7 Hulopoe Beach
7A Pool Grille
7B Ihilani
8A Munro Trail
8B The Challenge at Manele
8C The Experience at Koele
8D Hulopoe Court

Where to Stay
7A Four Seasons Resort at Manele Bay
5 Hotel Lanai
8D The Lodge at Koele

Where to Dine
5 Henry Clay's Rotisserie
6 Blue Ginger Café
7B Ihilani
7A Ocean Grill
9 Pele's Other Garden

Three days is ideal for Lanai. This is enough time to explore the island, relax on the beach, and engage in an activity, such as hiking to the top of the island, indulging in some of Hawaii's best scuba diving and snorkeling, or teeing off on one of Lanai's two resort golf courses. START: **Lanai City. Trip length: 85 miles (137km).**

Travel Tips

See the box on p 152 for information on getting to and around Lanai. Generally you will not need a car if you are staying at one of the two resorts or at the Hotel Lanai (they provide shuttle bus service), but exploring Lanai's many back roads is a fantastic opportunity to go four-wheeling. Make sure to grab a picnic lunch from Pele's Other Garden (p 158) before you head out of Lanai City.

Go north on Lanai Avenue from the car rental location, then right on Hwy. 430 (Keomuku Hwy.). Turn left on Poliha Road, just behind the stables and before the tennis courts (look for the rock sign that says GARDEN OF THE GODS). The next 26 miles (42km) is on dirt jeep trails and will take 60 to 75 minutes all the way down to the beach.

1 ★★ kids **Polihua Beach.** Lanai's largest white-sand beach is a

great spot to begin your journey. The beach's strong currents are generally not safe for swimming, and it can be windy, but the beach will probably be deserted and you'll have a great view of Molokai in the distance. So many sea turtles once hauled themselves out of the water to lay their eggs in the sun-baked sand on Lanai's northwestern shore that Hawaiians named the beach here Polihua, or "egg nest." Although the endangered green sea turtles are making a comeback, they're seldom seen here now. You're more likely to spot an off-shore whale (in season) or the perennial litter that washes up onto this deserted beach. There are no facilities, so bring water and sunscreen. Relax for a couple of hours, eat lunch, and walk the beach looking for shells.

Retrace your route back on Polihua Road about 12 miles (19km) and 45 minutes.

2 ★★ kids **Garden of the Gods.** See p 151, **2**.

Polihua Beach.

A sign in Lanai City.

Continue another 5 miles (8km) on Polihua Road.

③ ★ kids Kanepuu Preserve. Stop and take this self-guided nature trail, about a 10- to 15-minute walk through eight stations, with interpretive signs explaining the natural or cultural significance of what you're seeing. Kanepuu is one of the last remaining examples of the type of forest that once covered the dry lowlands throughout the state. There are some 49 plant species here that are found only in Hawaii.

Retrace your steps back to Lanai City.

④ ★★ kids Lanai City. See p 153, **⑤** for a description of this tiny village.

Plan to have dinner at an old-fashioned country lodge dining room, ⑤ ★ kids Lanai City Grill. Celebrated Maui chef Bev Gannon redesigned the menu in this cute eatery, where the decor consists of pine-paneled walls, chintz curtains, and a fireplace. The menu sticks to food that's in season and fresh that day. See p 158.

Start your second day with breakfast at tiny ⑥ Blue Ginger Café; my favorite is the homemade French toast. Order a second cup of coffee and sit and chat awhile with the locals; introduce yourself and ask them questions about Lanai. See p 158.

From Lanai City take Hwy. 440 (Kaumalapau Hwy.). Turn left at Manele Road, where Hwy. 440 continues. Continue to the end at Hulupoe Beach Park. Allow 30 to 35 minutes for the 11-mile (18km) trip.

⑦ ★★★ kids Hulopoe Beach. For your second day, plan to laze around Hulopoe Beach. Bring a good book, watch the kids play in the surf, or take a long slow walk around the crescent-shaped bay. Wander over to the Four Seasons–Lanai at Manele Bay for lunch poolside at the **⑦A Ocean Grill ★** (p 158), where the smoked scallop salad is "onolicious," as we say in Hawaii. Splurge on dinner: Book a table at **⑦B Ihilani** (p 158), with a view of the sun sinking into the ocean and indulge in the exquisite Italian cuisine (I recommend the lobster risotto). Be sure to save room for dessert.

Those wanting to hike or drive the Munro Trail, the well-marked trail begins at Lanai Cemetery along Keomoku Road (Hwy. 430). If you are interested in taking the Trilogy sail-snorkel trip, the boat leaves from Manele Boat Harbor. (From Lanai City take Hwy. 440/Kaumalapau Hwy., and continue to the end of the road. Allow 30–35 min. for the 11-mile/18km trip.) The Experience at Koele Golf Course is next-door to the Lodge at Koele in Lanai City; and the Challenge at Manele is next door

to the Four Seasons–Lanai at Manele Bay.

⑧ Adventures on Land or Water. On your third day, if it hasn't been raining and the ground is dry, do a little exploring. Here are a few options: The truly ambitious can spend the day (plan on at least 7 hr.) climbing to the top of Lanai at Lanaihale on the **⑧A ★★★ Munro Trail.** This tough, 11-mile (18km) (round-trip) uphill climb through groves of Norfolk pines begins at Lanai Cemetery along Keomoku Road (Hwy. 430). It's a lung buster, but if you reach the top, you'll be rewarded with a breathtaking view of Molokai, Maui, Kahoolawe, the peaks of the Big Island, and—on a really clear day—Oahu in the distance. The trail follows Lanai's ancient caldera rim, ending up at the island's highest point, Lanaihale. Go in the morning for the best visibility.

After 4 miles (6.4km), you'll get a view of Lanai City. If you're tired, you can retrace your steps from here, otherwise, continue the last 1.25 miles (2km) to the top. Die-hards can head down Lanai's steep south-crater rim to join the highway to Manele Bay. Soak in a hot tub on

your return. If you'd rather go out on (or into) the water, contact **Trilogy Lanai Ocean Sports ★★★** (☎ 888/MAUI-800 [628-4800]; www.visitlanai.com) about their sailing-snorkeling, whale-watching, or scuba trips. Golfers can head for either the **⑧B Challenge at Manele ★★★** (next to the Four Seasons–Lanai at Manele in Hulopoe Bay; ☎ 800/321-4666; greens fees $225 or $220 for resort guests), a target-style, desert-links course, designed by Jack Nicklaus, and one of the most challenging in the state; or **⑧C Experience at Koele ★★** (the Lodge at Koele in Lanai City; ☎ 800/321-4666; greens fees $225 or $220 for lodge guests), a traditional par-72 course, designed by Greg Norman with very different front and back 9 holes.

If you have time, have dinner in Lanai City at **⑧D Hulopoe Court** (p 158) in the Lodge at Koele. I recommend the steamed Hawaiian seafood *laulau* (with mahimahi, sea bass, shrimp, Molokai sweet potatoes, and local vegetables), grilled *opakapaka* with Lanai greens and a mango sauce, and Hawaiian-style short ribs and roast pork loin.

Munro Trail.

Where to Stay & Dine

Blue Ginger Café LANAI CITY *COFFEE SHOP*   This is a casual, inexpensive alternative to Lanai's fancy hotel restaurants. Try the popular hamburgers on homemade buns. *409 7th St. (at Ilima St.), Lanai City.* ☎ *808/565-6363. Breakfast and lunch items under $15; dinner entrees under $16. No credit cards. Breakfast, lunch & dinner Thurs–Mon; breakfast & lunch Tues–Wed. Map p 154.*

★ **Four Seasons Resort Lanai, The Lodge at Koele** LANAI CITY   This lodge resembles a grand English country estate and is in the cool mist of the mountains, 8 miles (13km) inland from any beach. *Lanai City.* ☎ *800/321-4666. www.fourseasons. com/lanai. 102 units. Doubles $345–$600. AE, DC, MC, V. Map p 154.*

★★★ kids **Four Seasons Resort at Manele Bay** HULOPOE BAY   This hotel steps down the hillside to one of Hawaii's best stretches of golden sand. Most of the spacious airy rooms open to breathtaking views. *Hulopoe Beach.* ☎ *800/321-4666. www.fourseasons.com/lanai. 236 units. Doubles $445–$645. AE, DC, MC, V. Map p 154.*

★ kids **Hotel Lanai** LANAI CITY   This hotel is perfect for families and other vacationers who are looking for a good deal. Built in the 1920s, it's a clapboard plantation-era relic that has retained its quaint character. *828 Lanai Ave., Lanai City.* ☎ *800/795-7211. www.hotellanai.com. 11 units. Doubles $159–$229 with breakfast. AE, MC, V. Map p 154.*

★★★ **Ihilani** HULOPOE BAY *ITALIAN*   This classy dining room serves a range of well-prepared dishes that includes an inspired lobster risotto.

In the Four Seasons–Lanai at Manele Bay. ☎ *808/565-2296. Set menu 2 courses with dessert $58, 3 courses $66, 3 courses with dessert $78. AE, DC, MC, V. Dinner Tues–Sat. Map p 154.*

★★ kids **Lanai City Grill** LANAI CITY *COUNTRY CUISINE*   Celebrated Maui chef Bev Gannon redesigned the menu in this cute eatery, where the decor consists of pine-paneled walls, chintz curtains, and a fireplace. The menu features seasonal and local ingredients. *In the Hotel Lanai. 828 Lanai Ave., Lanai City.* ☎ *808/565-7211. www.hotellanai.com. Entrees $28–$40. MC, V. Dinner Wed–Sun. Map p 154.*

★★ **Pele's Other Garden** LANAI CITY *DELI/BISTRO*   This popular eatery has grown from a small sandwich shop into a full-scale deli and bistro. Daily soup and menu specials, fresh organic produce, and special items make Pele's Other Garden a Lanai City must. *811 Houston St., Lanai City.* ☎ *808/565-9628. Entrees $7–$12 lunch, $14–$20 dinner; pizza from $7. AE, DISC, MC, V. Lunch Mon–Sat; lunch & dinner. Map p 154.*

★ **Ocean Grill** HULOPOE BAY SEAFOOD   Located just off the pool in the *Four Seasons–Lanai at Manele Bay*, this open-air bistro serves interesting lunches. At dinner, watch the sun set and the stars come out as you dine on entrees such as Hawaiian kampachi and red-curry chowder. *In the Four Seasons–Lanai at Manele Bay.* ☎ *808/565-2092. Entrees $14–$20 lunch, $31–$48 dinner. AE, DC, MC, V. Lunch daily; dinner Thurs–Mon. Map p 154.* ●

The
Savvy Traveler

Before You Go

Government Tourist Offices

On Maui: Maui Visitors Bureau (1727 Wili Pa Loop, Wailuku, HI 96793; ☎ 800/525-MAUI [6284]; www.visit maui.com). On Lanai: Lanai Visitors Bureau (P.O. Box 631436, Lanai City, HI 96763; ☎ 800/947-4774; www. visitlanai.net).

The Best Times to Go

Most visitors don't come to Maui when the weather's best in the islands; rather, they come when it's at its worst everywhere else. Thus, the high season—when prices are up and resorts are booked to capacity—generally runs from mid-December through March or mid-April. The last 2 weeks of December in particular are the prime time for travel to Maui. If you're planning a holiday trip, make your reservations as early as possible, count on holiday crowds, and expect to pay top dollar for accommodations, car rentals, and airfare. Whale-watching season begins in December and continues through the rest of winter, sometimes lasting into May.

The off seasons, when the best rates are available, spring (mid-Apr to mid-June) and fall (Sept to mid-Dec), are also Maui's best seasons in terms of reliably great weather. If you're looking to save money, or if you just want to avoid the crowds, this is the time to visit. Hotel rates and airfares tend to be significantly lower and good package deals are often available.

Note: If you plan to come to Maui between the last week in April and the first week in May, be sure to book your accommodations, inter-island air reservations, and car rental in advance. In Japan, the last week of April is called Golden Week,

Previous page: Driving the Kula Highway.

because three Japanese holidays take place one after the other. The islands are especially busy with Japanese tourists during this time.

Due to the large number of families traveling in summer (June–Aug), you won't get the fantastic bargains of spring and fall. However, you'll still do much better on packages, airfare, and accommodations than you will in winter.

Festivals & Special Events

WINTER. **Holiday Lighting of the Banyan Tree** is when Lahaina's historic Banyan Tree is lit up with thousands of Christmas lights in early December (☎ *888/310-1117; www. visitlahaina.com*). The end of December and early January brings the Academy of Motion Pictures' major screenings of top films with the **First Light,** at the Maui Arts and Cultural Center (☎ *808/579-9996; www.mauifilmfestival.com*). To celebrate **Chinese New Year** (Jan–Feb), the historic Wo Hing Temple in Lahaina town holds a traditional lion dance plus fireworks, food booths, and a host of activities (☎ *888/310-1117; www.visitlanai.net*). **Maui Whale Festival,** in February, is a month-long celebration on Maui with a variety of activities ranging from a parade, to crafts fairs, games, and food (☎ *808/249-8811; www.visitmaui.com*).

SPRING. In mid-March, the entire town of Lahaina celebrates **Ocean Arts Festival,** in Banyan Tree Park, with Hawaiian musicians and hula troupes, marine-related activities, games, and a "creature feature" touch-pool exhibit for children (☎ *888/310-1117; www.visitlahaina. com*). At the end of March or in

April, Hana holds the **East Maui Taro Festival,** serving taro in many different forms, from poi to chips. Also on hand are Hawaiian exhibits, demonstrations, and food booths (☎ 808/248-8972; www.calendar maui.com). Easter weekend brings the **Annual Ritz-Carlton Kapalua Celebration of the Arts** with Maui artists providing free hands-on lessons (☎ 808/669-6200; www. celebrationofthearts.org). May 1 is the **Annual Lei Day Celebration** throughout the island, with lei-making contests, pageantry, arts and crafts, and concerts (☎ 808/875-4100; www.visitmaui.com). In early May, the **Maui Onion Festival** takes place in Whalers Village, Kaanapali, featuring everything you ever wanted to know about the sweetest onions in the world, plus the Maui Onion Cook-Off (☎ 808/661-4567; www.whalersvillage.com).

SUMMER. A state holiday on June 10, **King Kamehameha Day,** jump-starts the summer with a massive floral parade and hoolaulea (party) (☎ 888/310-1117; www.visitlahaina. com). Just before Father's Day weekend in June, the **Maui Film Festival** at the Wailea Resort features 5 days and nights of premieres and special films, along with traditional Hawaiian storytelling, chants, hula, and contemporary music (☎ 808/579-9996; www.mauifilmfestival.com). On the first Saturday in July, on Lanai, the **Pineapple Festival** celebrates Lanai's history of pineapple plantation and ranching and includes eating and cooking contests, entertainment, arts and crafts, food, and fireworks (☎ 808/565-7600; www.visitlanai. net). The **Fourth of July** is celebrated on Maui with various activities (☎ 800/525-MAUI [6284]; www.visit maui.com). Throughout June and July, various Buddhist churches celebrate **Bon Dance and Lantern Ceremony,** a colorful ceremony honoring

the souls of the dead (☎ 808/661-4304; www.visitmaui.com). In early July, famous wine and food experts and oenophiles gather at the **Kapalua Wine and Food Festival** (☎ 800/ KAPALUA [527-2582]; www.kapalua resort.com), for tastings, panel discussions, and samplings of new releases.

FALL. The statewide **Aloha Festivals** (☎ 800/852-7690; www.alohafestivals. com), a series of celebrations, parades, and other events honoring the Hawaiian culture, takes place in September and October. Early September brings **A Taste of Lahaina,** where Maui's premier chefs serve up 40 signature entrees. The event includes cooking demonstrations, wine tastings, and live entertainment (☎ 888/310-1117; www.visitlahaina.com).

The Weather

Because Maui lies at the edge of the tropical zone, it technically has only two seasons, both of them warm. The dry season corresponds to summer, and the rainy season generally runs from November to March. The rainy season can cause gray weather and spoil your tanning opportunities. Fortunately, it seldom rains for more than 3 days straight, and rainy days often just consist of a mix of clouds and sun, with very brief showers.

The year-round temperature usually varies no more than 15 degrees, but it depends on where you are. Maui's leeward sides (the west and south) are usually hot and dry, whereas the windward sides (east and north) are generally cooler and moist. If you want arid, desertlike weather, go leeward. If you want lush, often wet, junglelike weather, go windward. Your best bets for total year-round sun are the Kihei-Wailea and Lahaina-Kapalua coasts.

Maui is also full of microclimates, thanks to its interior valleys, coastal

LAHAINA-KAANAPALI'S AVERAGE TEMPERATURE & RAINFALL

	JAN	FEB	MAR	APR	MAY	JUNE
Daily High (°F/°C)	82/28	80/27	83/28	84/29	85/29	87/31
Daily Low (°F/°C)	64/18	6317	64/18	65/18	67/19	68/20
Water Temp	75/24	74/23	74/23	75/24	76/24	77/25
Rain in Inches	3.5	2.4	1.8	1.1	1.1	0.1

	JULY	AUG	SEPT	OCT	NOV	DEC
Daily High (°F/°C)	88/31	88/31	89/32	88/31	86/30	83/28
Daily Low (°F/°C)	69/21	69/21	70/21	69/21	67/19	65/18
Water Temp	78/26	79/26	80/27	79/26	77/25	76/24
Rain in Inches	0.2	0.2	0.3	1.1	2.2	3.2

KIHEI-WAILEA'S AVERAGE TEMPERATURE & RAINFALL

	JAN	FEB	MAR	APR	MAY	JUNE
Daily High (°F/°C)	81/27	81/27	83/28	84/29	85/29	87/31
Daily Low (°F/°C)	63/17	63/17	64/18	64/18	65/18	67/19
Water Temp	75/24	74/23	74/23	75/24	76/24	77/25
Rain in Inches	4.1	2.9	2.7	1.8	0.8	0.3

	JULY	AUG	SEPT	OCT	NOV	DEC
Daily High (°F/°C)	8831	89/32	88/31	87/31	85/29	82/28
Daily Low (°F/°C)	69/21	69/21	69/21	68/20	67/19	65/18
Water Temp	78/26	79/26	80/27	79/26	77/25	76/24
Rain in Inches	0.4	0.5	0.4	1.3	2.6	3.3

plains, and mountain peaks. If you travel into the mountains, it can change from summer to winter in a matter of hours, because it's cooler the higher up you go.

Useful Websites

- **www.visitmaui.com**: The Maui Visitors Bureau's all-around guide to Maui and Lanai.
- **www.hawaiiradiotv.com/puka. html**: Hawaii's radio and television guide.
- **www.planet-hawaii.com**: An island guide to activities, lodging, shopping, culture, the surf report, weather, and more.
- **www.islandcurrents.com**: Specializes in arts and culture.
- **www.maui.net**: Directory of links to accommodations, activities, and shopping.
- **www.geocities.com/~olelo**: Hawaiian language website with easy lessons on Hawaiian and a cultural calendar.
- **www.visitlanai.net**: Lanai Visitors Bureau's website with information on the island of Lanai.
- **www.weather.com**: Up-to-the-minute worldwide weather reports.

Restaurant & Activity Reservations

Book well in advance if you're determined to eat at a particular spot or participate in a certain activity (like the Trilogy sailing-snorkeling trip to Lanai or scuba diving around Molokini). For popular restaurants, if you didn't call in advance, try asking for early or late hours—often tables are available before 6:30pm and after 9pm. You could also call the day before or first thing in the morning, when you may be able to take advantage of a cancellation.

Cellphones
In general it's a good bet that your cellphone will work in Maui, although coverage may not be as good as in your hometown. Cell coverage on Lanai may be spotty (few towers). If you're not from the U.S., you'll be appalled at the poor reach of the GSM (Global System for Mobiles) wireless network, which is used by much of the rest of the world. (To see where GSM phones work in the U.S., check out www.t-mobile.com/coverage/national_popup.asp.) Assume nothing—call your wireless provider and get the full scoop. In a worst-case scenario, you can always rent a phone from InTouch USA (☎ 800/872-7626; www.intouchglobal.com), but be aware that you'll pay $1 a minute or more for airtime.

Getting **There**

By Plane
If possible, fly directly to Maui. Doing so can save you a 2-hour layover in Honolulu and another plane ride. If you're headed for Lanai, you'll have to connect through Honolulu.

If you think of the island of Maui as the shape of a person's head and shoulders, you'll probably arrive on its neck, at **Kahului Airport.**

As of press time, the following airlines fly directly from the U.S. mainland to Kahului: **United Airlines** offers daily nonstop flights from San Francisco and Los Angeles; **Hawaiian Airlines** has direct flights from San Diego, Portland, and Seattle; **Alaska Airlines** offers flights from Anchorage to Seattle to Kahului; **American Airlines** flies direct from Los Angeles and San Jose; and **Delta Air Lines** offers direct flights from San Francisco via Los Angeles.

The other carriers—including Continental Airlines and Northwest Airlines—fly to Honolulu, where you'll have to pick up an interisland flight to Maui. (The airlines listed in the paragraph above also offer many more flights to Honolulu from additional cities on the mainland.) Hawaiian Airlines offers jet service from Honolulu.

In 2008, Hawaii lost one of its major interisland carriers, Aloha Airlines, but three carriers still remain: **Hawaiian Airlines** (☎ 800/367-5320; www.hawaiianair.com); **Mokulele Airlines** ☎ 866/260-7070; www.mokuleleairlines.com and **go!** (☎ 888/I-FLY-GO-2 [435-9462]; www.iflygo.com).

Visitors to Lanai have the following commuter airlines to choose from: **Mokulele Airlines** ☎ 866/260-7070; www.mokuleleairlines.com; go! (☎ 888/I-FLY-GO-2 [435-9462]; www.iflygo.com), **Pacific Wings' PW Express** services (☎ 888/866-5022 or 808/873-0877; www.flypwx.com), with daily nonstop flights between Honolulu and Molokai and Lanai, plus flights from Kahului, Maui. And **Island Air** (☎ 800/323-3345 or 808/484-2222; www.islandair.com) serves Hawaii's small interisland airports on Maui, Molokai, and Lanai. However, I have to warn you that I have not had stellar service on Island Air.

Getting **Around**

By Car

The only way to get around Maui is to rent a car. There is no real public transportation on Maui. The best way to get a good deal on a car rental is to book online. Maui's car-rental rates run about $47 a day (including all state taxes and fees). Cars are usually plentiful, except on holiday weekends, which in Hawaii also means King Kamehameha Day (June 11), Prince Kuhio Day (Mar 26), and Admission Day (3rd Fri in Aug). Rental cars are usually at a premium on Lanai, so book well ahead.

All the major car-rental agencies have offices on Maui: **Alamo** (☎ 800/327-9633; www.goalamo.com), Avis (☎ 800/321-3712; www.avis.com), **Budget** (☎ 800/572-0700; www.budget.com), **Dollar** (☎ 800/800-4000; www.dollarcar.com), **Hertz** (☎ 800/654-3011; www.hertz.com), and **National** (☎ 800/227-7368; www.nationalcar.com).

There are also a few frugal car-rental agencies offering older cars at discount prices. **Word of Mouth Rent-a-Used-Car** (☎ 800/533-5929 or 808/877-2436; www.mauirentacar.com) has used, older vehicles and requires a 4-day minimum rental. Rates start at $28 a day, with free airport pickup and drop-off included. **Maui Cruisers,** in Wailuku (☎ 877/749-7889 or 808/249-2319; www.mauicruisers.net), also offers free airport pickup and return on their older, used vehicles; rentals start at $28 a day (3-day minimum)

or $161 a week (including tax and insurance).

To rent a car in Hawaii, you must be at least 25 years old and have a valid driver's license and a credit card.

One more thing on car rentals: Hawaii is a no-fault state, which means that if you don't have collision-damage insurance, you are required to pay for all damages before you leave the state, whether or not the accident was your fault. Your personal car insurance back home may provide rental-car coverage; read your policy or call your insurer before you leave home. Bring your insurance identification card if you decline the optional insurance, which usually costs from $12 to $20 a day. Obtain the name of your company's local claim representative before you go. Some credit card companies also provide collision-damage insurance for their customers; check with yours before you rent.

By Taxi

You'll see taxis outside the airport terminal, but note that they are quite expensive—expect to spend around $60 to $75 for a ride from Kahului to Kaanapali and $50 from the airport to Wailea. For islandwide 24-hour service, call **Alii Cab Co.** (☎ 808/661-3688 or 808/667-2605). You can also try **Kihei Taxi** (☎ 808/879-3000), **Wailea Taxi** (☎ 808/874-5000), or **Maui Central Cab** (☎ 808/244-7278).

Fast **Facts**

ATMS Hawaii pioneered the use of **ATMs** nearly 3 decades ago, and now they're everywhere. You'll find them at most banks, in supermarkets, and in most resorts and shopping centers. **Cirrus** (☎ 800/424-7787;

www.mastercard.com) and **PLUS** (☎ 800/843-7587; www.visa.com) are the two most popular networks; check the back of your ATM card to see which network your bank belongs to (most banks belong to both these days).

BABYSITTING The first place to check is with your hotel. Many hotels have babysitting services or will provide you with lists of reliable sitters. You can also call **People Attentive to Children** (PATCH; ☎ 808/242-9232; www.patchhawaii.org), which will refer you to individuals who have taken their training courses on child care. If you are traveling to Lanai, call ☎ 800/498-4145.

BANKING HOURS Bank hours are Monday through Thursday from 8:30am to 3pm, Friday from 8:30am to 6pm; some banks are open on Saturday.

B&BS The top reservations service for bed-and-breakfasts is **Hawaii's Best Bed & Breakfasts** (☎ 800/262-9912; www.bestbnb.com).

BUSINESS HOURS Most offices are open from 8am to 5pm. Shopping centers are open Monday through Friday from 10am to 9pm, Saturday from 10am to 5:30pm, and Sunday from 10am to 5 or 6pm.

CLIMATE See "The Weather" on p 161.

CONCERTS See chapter 10, p 141.

CONDOMINIUM & VACATION HOME RENTALS For condos, I recommend **Bello Realty** (☎ 800/541-3060; www.bellomauivacations.com); for vacation rentals, contact **Hawaiian Beach Rentals** (☎ 800/853-0787; www.hawaiianbeachrentals.com) or **Hawaii Condo Exchange** (☎ 800/442-0404; http://hawaiicondo exchange.com).

CONSULATES & EMBASSIES All embassies are located in Washington, D.C. If your country isn't listed, call for directory information in Washington, D.C. (☎ 202/555-1212), for the number of your national embassy. The embassy of **Australia** is at 1601 Massachusetts Ave. NW, Washington, DC 20036 (☎ 202/797-3000; www.austemb.org). The embassy of **Canada** is at 501 Pennsylvania Ave. NW, Washington, DC 20001 (☎ 202/682-1740; www.canadianembassy.org). The embassy of **Ireland** is at 2234 Massachusetts Ave. NW, Washington, DC 20008 (☎ 202/462-3939; www.irelandemb.org). The embassy of the **United Kingdom** is at 3100 Massachusetts Ave. NW, Washington, DC 20008 (☎ 202/588-7800; www.britainusa.com/consular/embassy).

CREDIT CARDS Credit cards are a safe way to "carry" money; they provide a convenient record of all your expenses, and they generally offer good exchange rates. You can also withdraw cash advances from your credit cards at banks or ATMs, provided you know your PIN.

CUSTOMS Visitors arriving by air, no matter what the port of entry, should cultivate patience and resignation before setting foot on U.S. soil. Getting through customs and immigration control can take as long as 2 hours on some days. Travelers arriving from Canada will clear immigration and customs at their city of departure, which is much quicker.

DENTISTS If you have dental problems, a nationwide referral service known as 1-800-DENTIST (☎ 800/336-8478) will provide the name of a nearby dentist or clinic. Emergency dental care is available at **Kihei Dental Center** (1847 S. Kihei Rd., Kihei; ☎ 808/874-8401), or in Lahaina at the **Aloha Lahaina Dentists** (134 Luakini St., in the Maui Medical Group Bldg.; ☎ 808/661-4005).

DINING With a few exceptions at the high-end of the scale, dining attire is fairly casual. It's a good idea to make reservations in advance if you plan on eating between 7 and 9pm.

DOCTORS No appointment is necessary at **West Maui Healthcare Center,** Whalers Village (2435 Kaanapali Pkwy., Ste. H-7, near Leilani's Restaurant, Kaanapali; ☎ 808/667-9721), which is open 365 days a year until 10pm. In Kihei call **Urgent Care** (1325 S. Kihei Rd., Ste. 103, at Lipoa St., across from Star Market; ☎ 808/879-7781), which is open daily from 6am to midnight; doctors are on call 24 hours a day.

ELECTRICITY Like Canada, the United States uses 110 to 120 volts AC (60 cycles), compared to 220 to 240 volts AC (50 cycles) in most of Europe, Australia, and New Zealand. If your small appliances use 220 to 240 volts, you'll need a 110-volt transformer and a plug adapter with two flat parallel pins to operate them. Downward converters that change 220–240 volts to 110–120 volts are difficult to find in the United States, so bring one with you.

EMERGENCIES Dial ☎ 911 for the police, an ambulance, and the fire department. District stations are located in Lahaina (☎ 808/661-4441) and in Hana (☎ 808/248-8311). For the **Poison Control Center,** call ☎ 800/362-3585.

EVENT LISTINGS The best source for listings is the Friday edition of the local daily newspaper, **Maui News** (www.mauinews.com). There are also several tourist publications with listings, including **This Week on Maui** (www.thisweek.com) and **Maui Visitor Magazine** (www.visitormagazines.com). You can also check small, local community newspapers, such as **Maui Time Weekly** (www.mauitime.com); **Maui Weekly** (www.mauiweekly.com); **Lahaina News** (www.lahaina news.com); and the **Haleakala Times** (www.haleakalatimes.com).

FAMILY TRAVEL You might want to purchase a copy of **Frommer's Hawaii with Kids,** a guidebook dedicated to family visits to Hawaii. For family-friendly events, check out the Friday edition of the Maui News, the daily island newspaper, for events.

GAY & LESBIAN TRAVELERS The **International Gay & Lesbian Travel Association** (IGLTA; ☎ 800/448-8550 or 954/776-2626; www.iglta.org) is the trade association for the gay and lesbian travel industry and offers an online directory of gay- and lesbian-friendly travel businesses. For information on gay-friendly business, accommodations, and gay-owned and gay-friendly lodgings contact **Pacific Ocean Holidays** (P.O. Box 88245, Honolulu, HI 96830; ☎ 800/735-6600; www.gayhawaii.com).

HOLIDAYS Federal, state, and county government offices are closed on all federal holidays: January 1 (New Year's Day), third Monday in January (Martin Luther King Day), third Monday in February (Presidents' Day, Washington's Birthday), last Monday in May (Memorial Day), July 4th (Independence Day), first Monday in September (Labor Day), second Monday in October (Columbus Day), November 11 (Veterans Day), fourth Thursday in November (Thanksgiving Day), and December 25 (Christmas). State and county offices also are closed on local holidays, including Prince Kuhio Day (Mar 26), King Kamehameha Day (June 11), and Admission Day (third Fri in Aug). Other special days celebrated by many people in Hawaii but that do not involve the closing of federal, state, or county offices are Chinese New Year (in Jan or Feb), Girls' Day (Mar 3), Buddha's Birthday (Apr 8), Father Damien's Day (Apr 15), Boys' Day (May 5), Samoan Flag Day (in Aug),

Aloha Festivals (Sept or Oct), and Pearl Harbor Day (Dec 7).

INSURANCE Trip-cancellation insurance helps you get your money back if you have to back out of a trip, if you have to go home early, or if your travel supplier goes bankrupt. Allowed reasons for cancellation can range from sickness to natural disasters to the State Department declaring your destination unsafe for travel. In this unstable world, trip-cancellation insurance is a good buy if you're getting tickets well in advance. Insurance policy details vary, so read the fine print—and especially make sure that your airline or cruise line is on the list of carriers covered in case of bankruptcy. For information, contact one of the following insurers: **Access America** (☎ 866/807-3982; www.accessamerica.com), **Travel Guard International** (☎ 800/826-4919; www.travelguard.com), **Travel Insured International** (☎ 800/243-3174; www.travelinsured.com), and **Travelex Insurance Services** (☎ 888/457-4602; www.travelex-insurance.com).

Although it's not required of travelers, health insurance is highly recommended. Unlike many European countries, the United States does not usually offer free or low-cost medical care to its citizens or visitors. Doctors and hospitals are expensive, and in most cases will require advance payment or proof of coverage before they render their services. Though lack of health insurance may prevent you from being admitted to a hospital in non-emergencies, don't worry about being left on a street corner to die: The American way is to fix you now and bill the living daylights out of you later.

Insurance for British Travelers: Most big travel agents offer their own insurance and will probably try to sell you their package when you book a holiday. Think before you sign. Britain's Consumers' Association recommends that you insist on seeing the policy and reading the fine print before buying travel insurance. The **Association of British Insurers** (☎ 020/7600-3333; www.abi.org.uk) gives advice by phone and publishes *Holiday Insurance,* a free guide to policy provisions and prices. You might also shop around for better deals; try **Columbus Direct** (☎ 020/7375-0011; www.columbusdirect.net).

Insurance for Canadian Travelers: Canadians should check with their provincial health plan offices or call Health Canada (☎ 613/957-2991; www.hc-sc.gc.ca) to find out the extent of your coverage and what documentation and receipts you must take home in case you are treated in the United States.

Lost-Luggage Insurance: On domestic flights, checked baggage is covered *up to* $2,800 per ticketed passenger. Note the key words "up to," which does not mean you collect $2,800 if they lose your bag. When you read the fine print on your ticket, you often wonder what the heck they do cover as they explicitly state they have **NO** liability for damage or loss of protruding baggage parts (wheels, straps, pockets, pull handles, and so on), and **NO** liability for photographic equipment, computers, VCRs, and any other electronic equipment, including software or components, jewelry, cash, documents, furs, works of art, or other similar valuable items. On international flights (including U.S. portions of international trips), baggage liability is limited to $9.07 per pound ($20 per kg) or a maximum of 70 lb. (32kg), or $634.90, per checked bag. If you plan to check items more valuable than the standard liability, see if your valuables are covered by your homeowner's policy or get baggage insurance as part of your comprehensive travel-insurance package.

Don't buy insurance at the airport, as it's usually overpriced. Be sure to take any valuables or irreplaceable items with you in your carry-on luggage. If your luggage is lost, immediately file a lost-luggage claim at the airport, detailing the luggage contents (always carry a list in your carry on). For most airlines, you must report delayed, damaged, or lost baggage within 4 hours of arrival. The airlines are required to deliver luggage, once found, directly to your house or destination free of charge.

INTERNET ACCESS   Major hotels and even small B&Bs have Internet access; many of them have also have Wi-Fi. Just check the charges ahead of time, they can be exorbitant. The best Internet deal on Maui is in a **public library** (to find the closest location, check www.public libraries.com/hawaii.htm), which offers free access if you have a library card; a 3-month visitor card costs $10. In Kihei you can go to the **Hale Imua Internet Café,** in the Kamaole Center (☎ 808/891-9219). In Lahaina drop by **Buns of Maui** in the Old Lahaina Shopping Center (878 Front St.; ☎ 808/661-5407), which has the cheapest rates on Maui at only 8 cents a minute and no minimum.

MAIL & POSTAGE   To find the nearest post office, call ☎ 800/ASK-USPS [275-8777] or log on to www. usps.gov. In Lahaina the main post office is at the Lahaina Civic Center (1760 Honoapiilani Hwy.), in Kahului there's a branch at 138 S. Puunene Ave., and in Kihei there's one at 1254 S. Kihei Rd. Mail can be sent to you, in your name, c/o General Delivery, at the post office. Most post offices will hold your mail for up to 1 month. At press time, domestic postage rates were 28¢ for a postcard and 44¢ for a letter. For international mail, a first-class

letter of up to 1 ounce costs 75¢ and a first-class postcard costs 75¢.

MONEY   Don't carry a lot of cash in your wallet. Many small restaurants won't accept credit cards, so ask upfront if you plan to pay with plastic. Traveler's checks are something of an anachronism from the days before ATMs; **American Express** (☎ 800/221-7282), **Visa** (☎ 800/ 732-1322), and **MasterCard** (☎ 800/ 223-9920) all offer them. If you choose to carry traveler's checks, be sure to keep a record of their serial numbers separate from your checks in the event that they are stolen or lost.

PASSPORTS   Always keep a photocopy of your passport with you (but separate from your passport) when you're traveling. If your passport is lost or stolen, having a copy significantly facilitates the reissuing process at your consulate. Keep your passport and other valuables in your room's safe or in the hotel safe.

PHARMACIES   There are no 24-hour pharmacies on Maui. I recommend Longs Drugs stores (www.longs. com), which has two pharmacies: in Kihei (1215 S. Kihei Rd.; ☎ 808/879-2033), and in Kahului in the Maui Mall Shopping Center (70 E. Kaahumanu Ave.; ☎ 808/877-0068).

SAFETY   Although Hawaii is generally a safe tourist destination, visitors have been crime victims, so stay alert. The most common crime against tourists is rental-car break-ins. Never leave any valuables in your car, not even in your trunk. Be especially careful in high-risk areas, such as beaches and resorts. Never carry large amounts of cash with you. Stay in well-lighted areas after dark. Don't hike on deserted trails or swim in the ocean alone.

SENIOR TRAVELERS   Discounts for seniors are available at almost all of

Maui's major attractions, and occasionally at hotels and restaurants. Always inquire when making hotel reservations, and especially when you're buying your airline ticket—most major domestic airlines offer senior discounts. Members of **AARP** (☎ 800/424-3410 or 202/434-2277; www.aarp.org) are usually eligible for such discounts. AARP also puts together organized tour packages at moderate rates. Some great, low-cost trips to Hawaii are offered to people 55 and older through **Elderhostel** (75 Federal St., Boston, MA 02110; ☎ 617/426-8056; www.elderhostel.org), a nonprofit group that arranges travel and study programs around the world. You can obtain a complete catalog of offerings by writing to Elderhostel, P.O. Box 1959, Wakefield, MA 01880-5959. If you're planning to visit Haleakala National Park, you can save sightseeing dollars if you're 62 or older by picking up a **Golden Age Passport** from any national park, recreation area, or monument. This lifetime pass has a one-time fee of $10 and provides free admission to all of the parks in the system, plus a 50% savings on camping and recreation fees. Be sure to have proof of your age with you.

SPECTATOR SPORTS You've got your choice of **golf tournaments** (☎ 808/669-2440; www.kapaluamaui.com); **polo** (☎ 808/877-7744 or 808/572-7326; www.visitmaui.com); **Hawaiian outrigger canoe races,** from May to September (☎ 808/261-6615; www.y2kanu.com); **wind surfing** (☎ 808/877-2111); and **rodeo** (☎ 808/572-9565; www.visitmaui.com).

TAXES Hawaii's sales tax is 4%. Hotel occupancy tax is 7.25%, and the state allows hoteliers to tack on an additional .001666% excise tax. Thus, expect taxes of about 11.42% to be added to every hotel bill.

TAXIS See "Getting Around," earlier in this chapter.

TELEPHONE For directory assistance, dial ☎ 411; for long-distance information, dial 1, then the appropriate area code, and then 555-1212. Pay phones cost 50¢ for local calls (all calls on the island of Maui are local calls). The area code for all of Hawaii (not just Maui) is 808. Calls to other islands are considered long distance. For calls to other islands you have to dial 1 + 808 + the 7-digit phone number.

TIPPING Tipping is ingrained in the American way of life. Here are some rules of thumb: In hotels, tip bellhops at least $1 per bag ($2–$3 if you have a lot of luggage), and tip the chamber staff $1 to $2 per person per day (more if you've left a disaster area for him or her to clean up, or if you're traveling with kids and/or pets). Tip the doorman or concierge only if he or she has provided you with some specific service (like calling a cab). In restaurants, bars, and nightclubs, tip service staff 15% to 20% of the check, and tip bartenders 10% to 15%. Tipping is not expected in cafeterias and fast-food restaurants. Tip cab drivers 15% of the fare and tip skycaps at airports at least $1 per bag ($2–$3 if you have a lot of luggage).

TOILETS Your best bet is Starbucks or a fast-food restaurant. You can also head to hotel lobbies and shopping centers. Parks have restrooms, but generally they are not very clean and may be in need of major repairs.

TOURIST OFFICE See "Government Tourist Offices," earlier in this chapter.

TRAVELERS WITH DISABILITIES Travelers with disabilities are made to feel very welcome in Maui. Hotels are usually equipped with wheelchair-accessible rooms, and tour companies provide many special services. For more information contact the **Center for Independent Living Maui** (220 Imi Kala St., Ste. 103, Wailuku, HI 96793; ☎ 808/242-4966; TTY 808/242-4968; mcilogg@gte.net; no website). The only travel agency in Hawaii specializing in needs for travelers with disabilities is **Access Aloha Travel** (☎ 800/480-1143; www.accessalohatravel.com), which can book anything, including rental vans, accommodations, tours, cruises, airfare, and just about anything else you can think of. Travelers with disabilities who wish to do their own driving can rent hand-controlled cars from **Avis** (☎ 800/331-1212; www.avis.com) and **Hertz** (☎ 800/654-3131; www.hertz.com). The number of hand-controlled cars in Hawaii is limited, so be sure to book well in advance. For wheelchair-accessible vans, contact **Accessible Vans of Hawaii** (186 Mehani Circle, Kihei; ☎ 800/303-3750; www.accessiblevans.com). Maui recognizes other states' windshield placards indicating that the driver of the car has disabilities, so be sure to bring yours with you. Vision-impaired travelers who use a Seeing Eye dog need to present documentation that the dog is a trained Seeing Eye dog and has had rabies shots. For more information, contact the Animal Quarantine Facility (☎ 808/483-7171; www.hawaii.gov).

A Brief **History**

AROUND A.D. 700   Paddling outrigger canoes, the first ancestors of today's Hawaiians follow the stars and birds across the sea to Hawaii.

AROUND 1300   Transoceanic voyages halt; Hawaii begins to develop its own culture in earnest. The settlers build temples, fishponds, and aqueducts to irrigate taro plantations. Sailors become farmers and fishermen. Each island is a separate kingdom. The *alii* (chiefs) create a caste system and establish taboos. Violators are strangled. High priests ask the gods Lono and Ku for divine guidance. Ritual human sacrifices are common.

AROUND 1500   Piilani, from Hana, unites Maui, builds fishponds and irrigation fields, and begins creating a paved road some 4- to 6-feet (1.2–1.8km) wide around the entire island. Piilani's sons and his grandson complete the project.

1759   Kalaniopuu, a chief from the Big Island, captures Hana from the powerful Maui chief Kahikili, while Kahikili is busy overtaking Molokai. The Molokai chief escapes and flees with his wife to Hana, where the Big Island chief welcomes him. A few years later, the Molokai chief and his wife have a baby girl in Hana, named Kaahumanu, who later marries Kamehameha. During her lifetime, Kaahumanu makes major changes in Hawaii's culture, breaking the taboo against women eating with men and converting to Christianity. The latter leads the way for thousands of Hawaiians to adopt the religion of their queen.

1778   Captain James Cook sails into Waimea Bay on Kauai, where he is welcomed as the god Lono. Overnight, Stone Age Hawaii enters the age of iron. Nails are traded for freshwater, pigs, and the affections of Hawaiian women.

The sailors bring syphilis, measles, and other diseases to which the Hawaiians have no natural immunity, thereby unwittingly wreaking havoc on the native population.

FEBRUARY 14, 1779 Captain James Cook and four of his crew are killed in Kealakekua Bay on the Big Island.

1782 Kamehameha I begins his campaign to unify the Hawaiian islands.

1790 Using western weapons (guns and canons), Kamehameha successfully defeats (and slays) the warriors of Maui's chief Kahekili at Iao.

1795 Kamehameha finally conquers Maui, making Lahaina the capital of his new united kingdom.

1801 Kamehameha stops on Maui with his fleet of Pelehu war canoes on his way to do battle on Oahu and Kauai. He stays in Lahaina for a year, constructing the Brick Palace, Hawaii's first Western-style structure.

1810 Kamehameha I unites the Hawaiian Islands.

1819 Kamehameha I dies; his son Liholiho is proclaimed Kamehameha II. Under the influence of Queen Kaahumanu, Kamehameha II orders the destruction of *heiau* and an end to the *kapu* system, thus overthrowing the traditional Hawaiian religion. The first whaling ship, *Bellina,* drops anchor in Lahaina.

1823 Missionaries arrive in Lahaina from New England, bent on converting the pagans. The missionaries clothe the natives, ban them from dancing the hula, and nearly dismantle their ancient culture. They try to keep the whalers and sailors out of the bawdy houses, where whiskey flows freely and the virtue of native women is never safe.

1845 King Kamehameha III moves the capital of Hawaii from Lahaina to Honolulu, where the natural harbor can accommodate more commerce.

1849 George Wilfong, a sea captain, builds a mill in Hana and plants some 60 acres of sugar cane, creating Hawaii's first sugar plantation.

1876 An elaborate ditch system that takes water from rainy Haiku to the dry plains of Wailuku some 17 miles (27km) away cements the future of sugar in Maui.

JANUARY 17, 1893 A group of American sugar planters and missionary descendants, with the support of U.S. Marines, imprison Queen Liliuokalani in her own palace in Honolulu and illegally overthrow the Hawaiian government.

DECEMBER 7, 1941 Japanese Zeros bomb American warships based at Pearl Harbor, plunging the United States into World War II.

MARCH 18, 1959 Hawaii becomes the 50th state of the United States. The first jet airliners arrive, bringing 250,000 tourists to the fledgling state.

1960 Amfac, owner of Pioneer Sugar Company, builds Maui's first destination resort in Kaanapali.

1967 The state of Hawaii hosts 1 million tourists.

1975 Maui reaches the 1 million annual tourists mark. Ten years later the number is 2 million.

1990S Hawaii's economy goes into a tailspin following a series of events: First, the Gulf War severely curtails air travel to the island; then, Hurricane Iniki slams into Kauai, crippling its infrastructure; and finally, sugar-cane companies across the state began shutting down, laying off thousands of workers. Maui,

however, weathers this turbulent economic storm.

2009 Hawaii, the 50th state, celebrates 50 years of statehood.

The Hawaiian **Language**

Almost everyone here speaks English. But many folks in Hawaii speak Hawaiian as well. All visitors will hear the words aloha (hello/goodbye/love) and mahalo (thank you). If you've just arrived, you're a malihini. Someone who's been here a long time is a kamaaina. When you finish a job or your meal, you are pau (finished). On Friday it's pau hana, work finished. You eat pupu (Hawaii's version of hors d'oeuvres) when you go pau hana.

The Hawaiian alphabet, created by the New England missionaries, has only 12 letters: the 5 regular vowels (a, e, i, o, and u) and 7 consonants (h, k, l, m, n, p, and w). The vowels are pronounced in the Roman fashion, that is, ah, ay, ee, oh, and oo (as in "too")—not ay, ee, eye, oh, and you, as in English. For example, huhu is pronounced whowho. Most vowels are sounded separately, though some are pronounced together, as in Kalakaua (Kah-lah-cow-ah).

What Haole Means

When Hawaiians first saw Western visitors, they called the pale-skinned, frail-looking men haole because they looked so out of breath. In Hawaiian, ha means "breath," and ole means an absence of what precedes it. Today the term haole is generally a synonym for Caucasian or foreigner and is used without any intended disrespect. If uttered by an angry stranger who adds certain adjectives (like

"stupid"), the term can be construed as a racial slur.

Useful Words & Phrases
Here are some basic Hawaiian words that you'll often hear in Hawaii and see throughout this book. For a more complete list of Hawaiian words, go to www.geo cities.com/~olelo/hltableofcontents. html or www.hisurf.com/hawaiian/ dictionary.html.

alii Hawaiian royalty
aloha greeting or farewell
halau school
hale house or building
heiau Hawaiian temple or place of worship
kahuna priest or expert
kamaaina long-time Hawaii resident
kapa bark cloth
kapu taboo, forbidden
keiki child
lanai porch or veranda
lomilomi massage
mahalo thank you
makai a direction, toward the sea
mana spirit power
mauka a direction, toward the mountains
muumuu loose-fitting gown or dress
ono delicious
pali cliff
paniolo Hawaiian cowboy(s)
wiki quick

Pidgin: 'Eh Fo'Real, Brah
If you venture beyond the tourist areas, you might hear another local tongue: pidgin English, a

conglomeration of slang and words from the Hawaiian language. "Broke da mouth" (tastes really good) is the favorite pidgin phrase and one you might hear. "'Eh fo'real, brah" means "It's true, brother." You could be invited to hear an elder "talk story" (relating myths and memories). But because pidgin is really the province of the locals, your visit to Hawaii is likely to pass without your hearing much pidgin at all.

Eating in Maui

In the mid-1980s, Hawaii Regional Cuisine (HRC) ignited a culinary revolution. Culinary traditions from successive waves of Asian residents have resulted in unforgettable flavor combinations recalling Thai, Vietnamese, Japanese, Chinese, and Indo-Pacific roots. When combined with the fresh harvests from sea and land for which Hawaii is known, these ethnic and culinary traditions take on renewed vigor and a cross-cultural, yet uniquely Hawaiian, quality.

At the other end of the spectrum is the vast and endearing world of "local food." By that I mean plate lunches and poke, shave ice and saimin, bento lunches and manapua—cultural hybrids all. A plate lunch (Hawaii's version of high camp) is usually ordered from a lunch wagon and consists of fried mahimahi (or teriyaki beef or shoyu chicken), "two scoops rice," macaroni salad, and a few leaves of green, typically julienned cabbage. Heavy gravy is often the condiment of choice, accompanied by a soft drink in a paper cup or straight out of the can.

Another favorite is saimin—the local version of noodles in broth topped with scrambled eggs, green onions, and sometimes pork.

The bento, another popular quick meal available throughout Hawaii, is a compact, boxed assortment of picnic fare usually consisting of neatly arranged sections of rice, pickled vegetables, and fried chicken, beef, or pork.

From the plantations come manapua, a bready, doughy sphere filled with tasty fillings of sweetened pork or sweet beans. The daintier Chinese delicacy dim sum is made of translucent wrappers filled with fresh seafood, pork hash, and vegetables, served for breakfast and lunch. For dessert or a snack, the prevailing choice is shave ice, the island version of a snow cone.

A Hawaiian Seafood Primer
To help familiarize you with the menu language of Hawaii, here's a basic glossary of island fish:

ahi yellowfin or big-eye tuna
aku skipjack tuna
ehu red snapper
hapuupuu grouper, a sea bass
hebi spearfish
kajiki Pacific blue marlin, also called au
kumu goatfish
mahimahi dolphin fish (the game fish, not the mammal)
monchong bigscale or sickle pomfret
nairagi striped marlin, also called au
onaga ruby snapper
ono wahoo
opah moonfish
opakapaka pink snapper
papio jack trevally
shutome broadbill swordfish
tombo albacore tuna
uhu parrotfish
uku gray snapper
ulua large jack trevally

Airline & Car-Rental **Websites**

Airlines on Maui

AIR CANADA
www.aircanada.com

AMERICAN AIRLINES
www.aa.com

CONTINENTAL AIRLINES
www.continental.com

DELTA AIR LINES
www.delta.com

go!
www.iflygo.com

HAWAIIAN AIRLINES
www.hawaiianair.com

ISLAND AIR
www.islandair.com

MOKULELE AIRLINES
www.mokuleleairlines.com

NORTHWEST AIRLINES
www.nwa.com

UNITED AIRLINES
www.ual.com

WEST JET
www.westjet.com

Car-Rental Agencies on Maui

ALAMO
www.goalamo.com

AVIS
www.avis.com

BUDGET
www.budget.com

DOLLAR
www.dollarcar.com

HERTZ
www.hertz.com

MAUI CRUISERS
www.mauicruisers.net

NATIONAL
www.nationalcar.com

WORD OF MOUTH RENT-A-CAR
www.mauirentacar.com

Index

See also Accommodations and Restaurant indexes, below.

Photo **Credits**